T0312787

'A critical compass for all to rethink the Mid
what it could be. This is an ambitious charte
hope for a new generation, and generations to come.

—Lyse Doucet, Chief International Correspondent, BBC News

'A passionate and accurate analysis of the past and future of the Middle East,
showing that while tyranny persists after the 2011 uprisings, there is also
resilience and resistance. Offering a sound, creative path away from devastating
Western military intervention, this is a loud cry for profound transformation
by two prominent activists of the region.'

—Madawi Al-Rasheed, Fellow of the British Academy,
Visiting Professor at the LSE Middle East Centre, and author of
The Son King

'A rare genuine effort to provide an objective yet impassioned analysis of the
Middle East from inside the region. From 9/11 to the Arab Spring to ISIS and
countless ill-conceived foreign interventions, this book is essential reading for
understanding the cycle of violence and tyranny—and for breaking that cycle.'

—Garry Kasparov, Chairman of the Human Rights Foundation and the
Renew Democracy Initiative

'It is a tribute to Iyad El-Baghdadi and Ahmed Gatnash that this book makes
just as uncomfortable reading for Western politicians and policymakers as it
would for the Middle East's tyrants and terrorists. A brave, unflinching analysis
of a region bedevilled by crises, written not by another Western "expert" but
by two compelling Arab voices.'

—Justin Marozzi, author of *Islamic Empires: Fifteen Cities that
Define a Civilisation*

'Anyone who wants to understand the traumas of the contemporary Middle
East, and is willing to learn how deeply implicated in them the West is, must
read this book.'

—Peter Beinart, author of *The Crisis of Zionism*

'It took me a lifetime to try to understand why the region where I was born
and raised is a crisis factory. This book is a genuine guide, full of important
information, accurate context and honest hope for those who want to understand the Middle East.'

—Ghada Oueiss, Principal Presenter, Al Jazeera Arabic

'An astute geopolitical analysis that is also deeply heartfelt. The authors' discussion of tyranny, terrorism and foreign intervention in the Middle East is well researched and unsparing; their personal stories and hopes for the future (complete with practical suggestions) make it stand out.'

— Sarah Kendzior, author of *Hiding in Plain Sight and The View from Flyover Country*

'After decades of the West aiding and abetting authoritarianism across the Middle East, on 6 January 2021, a white supremacist mob attacked the seat of US democracy, aiming to install a dictator. In *The Middle East Crisis Factory*, two prominent activists sound the alarm that authoritarianism anywhere is a threat to democracy everywhere.'

— Rula Jebreal, award-winning author and journalist

THE MIDDLE EAST CRISIS FACTORY

IYAD EL-BAGHDADI
AHMED GATNASH

The Middle East Crisis Factory

Tyranny, Resilience and Resistance

HURST & COMPANY, LONDON

First published in the United Kingdom in 2021 by
C. Hurst & Co. (Publishers) Ltd.,
83 Torbay Road, London NW6 7DT
© Iyad El-Baghdadi and Ahmed Gatnash, 2021
All rights reserved.
Printed in the United Kingdom

Distributed in the United States, Canada and Latin America by
Oxford University Press, 198 Madison Avenue, New York, NY 10016,
United States of America.

The right of Iyad El-Baghdadi and Ahmed Gatnash to be identified as the
authors of this publication is asserted by them in accordance with the
Copyright, Designs and Patents Act, 1988.

A Cataloguing-in-Publication data record for this book
is available from the British Library.

ISBN: 9781787383043

This book is printed using paper from registered sustainable
and managed sources.

www.hurstpublishers.com

To Bassem, Jamal, Raed, and all our fallen heroes:

We will never forget
We will never forgive
And we will never stop fighting.
We fight for everyone
Nobody gets left behind
We're not free until we're all free
And we're not safe until we're all safe.

CONTENTS

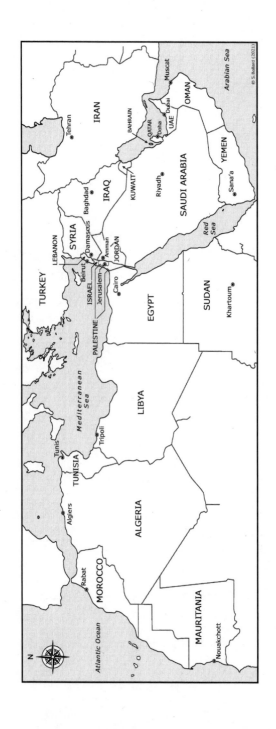

FOREWORD

Iyad El-Baghdadi

I did not expect this to be my first book.

* * *

On 17 December 2010, Mohamed Bouazizi, a young Tunisian street vendor, set himself on fire in a final act of protest against a life of daily humiliation and despair under a dictatorial regime. Within weeks, a fire had spread across the entire Arabic-speaking world, inspiring protests and defiance from a generation that had known nothing but tyranny, many having lived under the same ruler their entire lives. Over the next few months, the Arab Spring—as it came to be called—transformed my life, imbuing me with a sense of determination and responsibility.

I was then a thirty-three-year-old start-up consultant, born to Palestinian parents but raised in the United Arab Emirates. My friend and co-writer, Ahmed Gatnash, was a nineteen-year-old student watching his parents' country, Libya, erupt into revolution from afar, having been born and raised in the United Kingdom. The uprisings made life seem more hopeful and more purposeful, as if a historical window of opportunity had opened.

FOREWORD

When we started talking online in 2012, I told Ahmed that I was writing a manifesto in which I hoped to introduce a kind of left-libertarianism that I called Islamic libertarianism. That, I thought, would be my first book.

The window of opportunity wasn't open for long. The dictators would soon deliver a heavy blow to our revolutions' momentum, working to re-establish a status quo in which revolution was impossible and the people were forever subdued. Classical Arab powers such as Egypt fell to the status of mere vassals, as a new regional order arose, dominated by a counter-revolutionary axis with Riyadh and Abu Dhabi at its centre. Saudi Crown Prince Mohammad bin Salman, known by the initials MBS, quickly became the poster boy of this new phase of our region's history.

But the heyday of the counter-revolution didn't last forever, either. It too came to an end, and that transition brings its own painful memories. Trump's election in 2016 gave the counter-revolutionary axis an enormous boost; the world's most powerful country was now led by one of their cronies. The dictators felt invincible, but they also became extremely reckless, and their recklessness would eventually catch up with them.

On 2 October 2018, immediately after giving a lecture in Mainz, Germany, my friend and colleague Khaled Albaih told me that our friend Jamal Khashoggi—a prominent, Washington-based Saudi journalist—had mysteriously gone missing. Our dread grew every day, as we feared he had been kidnapped and taken back to Saudi Arabia. The truth would prove far worse than our darkest nightmares: Jamal was brutally murdered in his own country's consulate in Istanbul.

We viewed the aftermath of Jamal's killing differently from most Western commentators, who for years had tuned in and out of our region's politics depending on the mood in DC. For us, the most significant outcome was not that MBS proved his impunity or 'got away' with the murder, but rather that through this crime, he had ultimately broken his own back and jeopardised the entire project of the counter-revolutionary axis.

MBS was slated as a model for our region—the heroic, Western-friendly strongman who could 'open up' our stubbornly closed countries, bring 'reform' to our crooked ways, and fight the 'terrorism' that sprung from our lands. He had enjoyed stellar global PR up to that point, boosted by the orientalist narratives of powerful nations that had the audacity to describe themselves as leaders of a 'free' world.

When Jamal's murderers dismembered his body, they were not aware that they were also dismembering that mythical reformist leader whom so many desperately wanted to believe in. MBS went from being a model moderniser to the face of the single most gruesome political murder of a generation. The crown prince proved successful only in undermining the counter-revolution's credibility and irreparably wounding the idea of the 'strongman reformer'.

A new phase in our region's history was dawning, and it didn't take long for us to see the tides change. In December 2018, an uprising started in Sudan, its momentum steadily growing despite the counter-revolutionary axis's attempts to quell or co-opt it. In February 2019, an uprising began in Algeria that quickly escalated. In October 2019, radical protests broke out in Iraq, their participants demanding an end to corruption, unemployment, and oligarchy; two weeks later, protests broke out in Lebanon. In November, mass protests broke out in Iran.

The Khashoggi murder and its aftermath were not causal factors in any of these uprisings, and protesters in these countries probably didn't have MBS in mind when they took to the streets. But for observers, the link could not be ignored. The world was looking at these events, figuring out what to do, knowing that they couldn't pull the mythical 'reformer-autocrat' model on us ever again. Something was radically different this time around.

FOREWORD

Algeria's Abdelaziz Bouteflika was forced to resign on 2 April 2019; on 11 April, Sudan's Omar al-Bashir's thirty-year rule came to an end. In September, protests even broke out against Sisi in Egypt, taking analysts by surprise. Demonstrations continued in Algeria, Lebanon, Iraq, and Iran until the Covid-19 pandemic brought a stop to mass gatherings.

It has now been a decade since 2011, and the Middle East seems a darker, harsher, more dangerous, and less stable place. But underneath an ugly, blood-stained shell is something green, fresh, and beautiful struggling to push through. And as we step into a new decade, we renew our resolve to fight and build, build and fight, until it finds its way into the light.

* * *

My manifesto for an Islamic libertarianism was never completed, and my life would take several sharp turns. In April 2014, I was arrested by Emirati authorities and informed that there were 'higher orders' for my expulsion from the country where I had lived all my life. As a stateless Palestinian, I had nowhere to be returned to—so after a few weeks in jail, I was deported to Malaysia, where I spent the next month stranded in Kuala Lumpur International Airport. My journey would ultimately take me to Oslo, Norway, where, after a cold winter in a refugee camp, I was granted political asylum.

Personal stability would not come any time soon. In 2015, the rest of my family members had to leave the UAE, my father now broken and in poor mental health. In 2016, due to my assistance to native activists, ISIS placed my name on a hitlist, exhorting lone wolves to 'take action'; the next year, they delivered another threat. Then, in 2019, Norwegian intelligence agents showed up at my doorstep unannounced and took me away, informing me that I was a planned target of the Saudi regime's attacks against dissidents.

FOREWORD

Today I live under police protection in Oslo, aware that I'm as much a long-term problem to the tyrants and the terrorists as they are to me.

Welcome to the Crisis Factory

That was my personal journey—one of many taken by my comrades since, and before, 2011. For us, the region's politics are not just news on a screen—my family's safety is not 'politics'; my friends' lives aren't 'politics'. These are our lived realities; realities we didn't fully choose, but that we must overcome.

My move to Europe wasn't smooth, and life as a stateless refugee frequently got in the way of life as a writer and activist. But I was able to maintain an active presence on Twitter, and my audience continued to grow. I was frequently sought out for analysis and interviews, and I had countless conversations about the Middle East with journalists, think-tankers, politicians, foreign policy experts, and civil society activists. The big question is always, 'Why is the region so messed up, and how can it be fixed?'

To a Western politician tasked with dealing with the Middle East, our region may look distant, baffling, and hostile. Ronald Reagan's secretary of state, Alexander Haig, once described its history as 'one of failure and frustration, of feudalism and tribalism.' Reagan himself, in his 1990 memoirs, wrote: 'Perhaps we didn't appreciate fully enough the depth of the hatred and the complexity of the problems that made the Middle East such a jungle ... a suicide car bomber committing mass murder to gain instant entry to Paradise was so foreign to our own values and consciousness ... the irrationality of Middle Eastern politics forced us to rethink our policy there.'[1]

The irony seems to have escaped both Haig and Reagan, given how deeply Western foreign policy since the colonial era has contributed to making the Middle East the 'jungle' that it is; to a native, this sounds like a domestic abuser wondering why the household he battered for years is so dysfunctional. Only, this serial abuser seems genuinely oblivious, and actually thinks he's done nothing but good.

Barack Obama started his presidency with audaciously hopeful ideas about a different kind of relationship between the US and the wider Muslim world. In a speech in Cairo in 2009, he proclaimed: 'I've come here ... to seek a new beginning between the United States and Muslims around the world, one based upon mutual interest and mutual respect, and one based upon the truth that America and Islam ... share common principles—principles of justice and progress; tolerance and the dignity of all human beings.'[2] Yet seven years and many missteps later, as he ended his second term, his tone was far more cynical: 'The Middle East is going through a transformation ... rooted in conflicts that date back millennia.'[3]

Once again, it seems the irony went over Obama's head. The conflicts in the Middle East date back decades, not millennia; and his foreign policy choices poured gasoline on these conflicts even as the region was going through a historical intergenerational transformation.

For decades in the Middle East, one fact has remained constant, confirmed by successive opinion polls: Except for Israel, the region has remained intensely anti-Western, with America—as the flag-bearer of Western influence in the region—bearing the brunt of its people's dislike. Predictably, Trump's presidency only made matters worse—a 2017 Pew opinion poll found the Middle East to be the world's most intensely anti-American region, with the percentage of respondents who said they had a favourable opinion of the United States a mere 34 per cent in Lebanon, 27 per cent in Tunisia, and 18 per cent in Jordan.[4]

It wasn't always that way, though. In the 1919 Egyptian uprising, protesters marched carrying American flags next to Egyptian ones. At the time, many people in the Middle East looked upon the US very positively, especially since Wilson's '14 Points' emphasised the right to self-determination, which they saw as supportive of their struggle for independence from colonialism.

Decades before that, notable Syrian intellectual Abdulrahman Al-Kawaakibi wrote an appraisal of America in his 1902 book *The Nature of Tyranny*. Even as he acknowledged America's deep imperfections, he stressed that, compared to other contemporary governments, it had a political system that effectively restrained tyranny.

The people of the region are so starved of solidarity, and so regularly let down by both their own regimes and international institutions, that they're very grateful when they see expressions of support for their native agency. Unfortunately, such expressions are few and far between, and whatever historical windows of opportunity were opened in 2011 quickly closed, giving way to cynicism and disillusionment.

'Why is the Middle East so messed up, and how can it be fixed?' The problem starts with the question itself. Human societies are living, breathing things; you don't 'fix' living things, you heal them. The question should be more about what has hurt our societies and how we stop the hurt.

How This Book Came About

Having had a number of important conversations in the aftermath of the 2011 uprisings, Ahmed and I started working as a writing team in 2013, while he was based in the UK and I was in the UAE. After I was granted political asylum in Norway in 2015, working together became safer and easier, and we stepped up our collaboration.

Time and again, it seemed to us that a number of stubborn modes of thinking made it frustratingly difficult to get through to the average Westerner, even those committed to democracy and human rights, and sympathetic to our cause.

First is a tendency towards one-dimensional analyses of oppression in the Middle East. Some analysts focus on foreign intervention as the source, while others focus on terrorism, and others on authoritarian governments. We had repeatedly asserted that, in the Middle East, multiple systems of violence existed in a symbiotic relationship, each relying upon the others for sustainability.

Second is an inability to imagine a foreign policy that can take a strong stand for democracy without being militaristic. Cynicism cannot be an answer. At a 2017 conference in Berlin, a European speaker opened his presentation with photos of the aftermath of the Iraq War. 'Is democracy worth it? Is free speech worth the trash it produces?' he asked, as I squirmed in my seat, having lost a home and a past life for speaking out for democracy and free speech.

There seems to be a genuine impasse in thinking about foreign policy that makes being principled on human rights appear dogmatic and idealistic. It sets up our only choices as being muscular military adventures at one extreme, and playing nice with dictatorships in the hope of fostering 'reform' at another. We assert in this book that Western countries have a lot of leverage that they can exercise without having to resort to destructive military intervention. We also stress that strong societies are the best check on tyranny. If there is a way of achieving victory over tyrants, it is by empowering their own societies to resist them and clip their wings, or to be able to remove them altogether.

Third is a tendency to tie the structures of oppression in the Middle East to either culture or ideology, thus making them seem at once too opaque, too complex, and too intrinsic. We aim to challenge these conventional views and explore the themes of cultural fluidity and ideological change. A particular strain in mainstream thinking sees cultures and ideologies as fundamental, with narratives being the mere means by which ideology is disseminated. We should instead, perhaps, consider the opposite view—that narratives are more fundamental, more compelling, and more persistent, and that ideologies grow out of them as systems of justification. We will later explore interlocking narratives employed by tyrants, terrorists, and foreign interventions—narratives that find expression in a number of different ideologies, pushed by a number of groups.

This is a book about both the past and the future; about both freedom and tyranny. We wrote it to offer a framework to understand the Middle East's dilemmas, to explain its power dynamics, and to present solutions. We poured into it many years of frustration, but—in dedicating half of the book's chapters to the future—we believe that it is ultimately hopeful. We hope you will appreciate our humble effort to tell you our truth.

A note about how we refer to our region. Although we identify as Arab, we belong to a region that transcends ethnicity, religion, and language, home to many peoples who have coexisted throughout history and whose stories are intertwined. We use the terms 'Middle East' and 'MENA' (Middle East and North Africa) interchangeably in this book to refer to this expansive region. In light of our own areas of expertise and our lived experience, the narrative of this book focuses primarily on the region's Arabic-speaking portions, with Iran also featuring frequently in the case studies and analysis.

Let's now start with a reality check. Orientalist and essentialist assumptions make powerful blinkers that can prevent even smart and informed people from accessing our core messages, and we want to tackle them head on.

INTRODUCTION

AN UNLEARNING

To every complex question, there is usually an answer that is clear, simple, and wrong. In the face of the Middle East's perceived complexity come a number of oversimplifications that dig a deeper hole; some are a product of sheer laziness, while others reflect a bigoted condescension befitting nineteenth-century imperialists. Such 'answers' are worse than just wrong—they are toxic, and they feed a pessimism reflected in bad policies that end up further empowering the region's many bad actors.

Now, we'll be first to caution against the overuse of 'orientalism' by those who throw the term around to dismiss any critique of our region's shortcomings, whether social, cultural, or political (especially when this is done in defence of one's favourite partisan). But genuine orientalism does exist, and it is marked by an inability to take anything in 'the Orient' on its own terms, only viewing it in comparison or relation to the West. It is an exaggerated ethnocentrism that not only sets out to decide what is the 'proper' and 'normal' way to be, but even goes so far as to decide for the non-Western native who they are or what their region is. The opposite of this attitude is, simply, to humanise the region and its people and to see them as they are themselves.

It's been said that the enemy of knowledge isn't ignorance, but the illusion of knowledge. Many tropes do more than just misinform—they hinder people's access to understanding the region. And so, before diving into this book's ideas, we must first unlearn some bad ideas. Here are some of the tropes that we find particularly damaging.

No, it's not 'ancient hatreds'

One of the most frustrating beliefs out there is that the region's instability is the result of enmities between its constituent demographics that go back millennia. This amounts to an assertion that 'they've always been like that, and therefore it's pointless to ask why they behave this way and foolish to expect them to change any time soon'. Not only does this line essentialise—it also deliberately obfuscates the sources of today's conflicts, by presenting these conflicts as something inherent in the nature of the Middle East, rather than as things that have specific causes, often rooted in grievances and inequalities that can be understood as a human story before being a Middle Eastern or Arab one.

And what is most interesting about the 'ancient hatreds' line is the fact that, until very recently, it could have easily been applied just as well to Europe, whose various nations have fought each other for well over a millennium, and in the twentieth century alone gave us two World Wars that left over a hundred million dead. In fact, it can also be applied to, say, East Asia, with its long history of conflict between Japanese, Chinese, Koreans and Mongols; or even to the United States, with its history of racial conflict. Indeed, if you look at humanity's political history as a whole, the entire thing is a long-running record of violence.

Sure, you can connect any conflict in the world back to a previous one, ad infinitum, but most of the conflicts in the

Middle East are fairly modern, having modern sources reflecting existing grievances. And sure, identity politics can make one identify with a certain tribe and adopt their mythology, and with it, their historical grievances—but this is just what it is: mythology based upon identitarian narratives. The current Sunni–Shia conflict, for example, flared up in 2012, against the backdrop of events from 1979; to talk about it as the result of a seventh-century schism only obscures its modern origins. That isn't to deny that certain groups and demographics have been historically marginalised, but their marginalisation isn't anything essential to the groups themselves or to the region. Equality in our lifetimes is an achievable and worthwhile goal.

Not only is the 'ancient hatreds' line wrong—it also risks producing new hatreds between us and those peddling it. To some, it may be a convenient simplification; to many of us, it's deeply dehumanising. It's difficult to see eye to eye with someone when they're looking down on you—when, with a single sentence, they zoom out from the scale of years to the scale of millennia, making an entire generation's existence, with all its dreams and grievances, a mere detail in a story of inherent violence spanning the very history of civilisation.

The 'ancient hatreds' trope often reflects a condescending lack of curiosity about the region, and a desire to disengage from it, sometimes by the very parties that for decades caused immense damage to it through direct intervention or through the legitimisation of bad actors. This disengagement is not rooted in respect for the other's boundaries, but in a disdain for them and a pessimism about their prospects. When you think 'they've always been like this and can't change', it makes no sense to support their struggle for liberation or human rights. It makes far more sense, then, to find a friendly strongman to be your man in the tough neighbourhood.

No, we're not doomed to an eternal choice between tyranny and extremism

We have been engaged in debates about Islam and democracy for years, and this is unfortunately a common argument—not only in commentaries on current affairs, but also in discussions about whether Islam is 'compatible with democracy'. The argument goes that if Muslim-majority societies are allowed to vote, then what we will see is an Islamist takeover, and that the resulting states will not in fact be democratic, but rather authoritarian and anti-Western. It is best, then, that Western countries support the status quo of pro-Western authoritarians.

Two groups, for their own reasons, wish to deny us political agency and constantly boost this narrative: Islamophobes, and regional tyrants (of whom the UAE's Mohammad bin Zayed is a prime example).[1] They point to, for example, the Islamic Salvation Front winning Algeria's elections in 1991, Hamas winning Palestinian elections in 2006, and the Muslim Brotherhood's Freedom and Justice Party (FJP) winning the Egyptian elections in 2012.

This is not just a talking point peddled by fringe right-wing figures—similar arguments have been used by high-level American officials, including some in the Obama administration. In a 2018 article, David Kirkpatrick quotes John Kerry justifying American support for the 2013 coup that ended Egypt's democratic transition: 'It wasn't Jeffersonian democracy. ... Most of the time, this is the kind of government they had—almost all of the time. And the reality is, no matter how much I wish it was different, it ain't going to be different tomorrow.'[2] Somehow, we had to go from dictatorship to mature democracy in two years, or else lose our right to vote at all.

Do Muslim-majority societies always elect Islamists? Let's look at the facts. Islamists did win the 2012 elections in Egypt, but only narrowly so. In the election's first round, the two competing Islamist candidates received a total of 44.45 per cent of the vote; meanwhile the three main non-Islamist candidates received a total of 55.55 per cent. It is only thanks to the first-past-the-post electoral system, which forced a harsh choice between an ex-Mubarak regime figure and the Muslim Brotherhood candidate, that the late Mohamed Morsi was elected president.

Meanwhile, Islamist parties lost elections in Libya (2012), Tunisia (2014 and 2019), Malaysia (2018), and Indonesia (2019); in Turkey's 2019 local elections, the Islamist-leaning AKP party won a majority, but lost control of Istanbul, Turkey's largest city. At the same time, we've seen full-blown uprisings against political Islamist regimes in Iraq and Sudan, even as protests against the Islamic Republic of Iran continue.

The idea that Muslims will always prefer Islamists is simply not based on facts. Rather, Islamists sometimes win elections, and often lose.

Western observers make a serious error in judgment when they misunderstand the Islamist phenomenon, thinking that Islamists want to take us towards a theocratic governance model such as the Iranian regime. While political Islamists sometimes use the language of theocracy, the state that many of them envision would look less like a theocracy and more like an illiberal democracy. It would not look like present-day Iran, but rather like present-day Russia.

(While the Iranian regime's model has the upper hand in Iran and some support among Shia communities, it does not enjoy mass appeal. In fact, since 2019 we have witnessed Shia-led protests in Iraq against the Iranian regime's influence over Iraqi politics; not to mention the radical protests in Iran itself.)

Political Islamists should be understood not as theocrats but as right-wing populists. There are as many populisms as there are identities—Islamists are populists who weaponise the Islamic identity shared across the region. And like all populists, political Islamists are often effective in opposition and good at talking a big game, but once they take power, they rarely deliver for the average citizen who wants a better economy, a better health care system, less corruption, and better services.

The difference is that when right-wing populists are elected in Western nations and fail to deliver, they are simply voted out in a future election. But when Muslim nations elect Islamists, then the very idea of universal democratic rights is questioned. Many of us watched in horror during the 2016 attempted coup d'état in Turkey as hardened liberals seemed to repudiate their belief in democracy, cheering a potential military ousting of Erdoğan. One wonders, would they be as enthusiastic about a military coup against Hungary's Orbán or the UK's Boris Johnson?

It seems that only Western democracies have the right to elect right-wing populists without their very agency being called into question for 'making the wrong choice'. Nobody wondered whether Americans should have their democratic rights repealed after electing Donald Trump; in fact, many Europeans looked at Americans with sympathy rather than disgust. We can only imagine what the media narrative would have been had a privates-grabbing racist won free and fair elections in a major Muslim-majority country.

The appeal of populists is, in fact, the same across human societies. When people live in fear and anxiety in times of uncertainty, they look for strong, protective figures and seek comfort in the bosom of identity. It took a bit of economic anxiety over their loss of dominance for mostly white Americans to elect Donald Trump; meanwhile in the MENA region, after experiencing decades of massacres, bombings, terror waves, and occupations, the wonder is not that Muslim-majority societies sometimes elect Islamist populists, but rather that they often don't.

What it even means to be an Islamist is a question in flux. There has been a steady ideological transition among political

Islamists since 2011, which accelerated further after the 2014 rise of the 'Islamic State' forced many to sharply differentiate their own projects from the horrors of ISIS. Importantly, political Islamists no longer have a monopoly over religious discourse—many of those voting against them are religious Muslims who simply do not believe that Islamist parties are legitimate representatives of the values of their faith.

For democracy in the Middle East to work, Islamists must be brought into politics rather than pushed out of it. The more useful conversation to be had, both in the MENA and in the West, is about ensuring the integrity of democratic institutions against right-wing populists in power. The principle of democratic rights itself should never be questioned. In the words of our late friend Jamal Khashoggi, either we have a democracy in which Islamists can sometimes win elections, or we have dictatorships where there are no elections at all. They win, they fail, they get voted out; and the result is more political maturity among the electorate.

No, the region won't automatically get better if it's left alone

Some foreign powers have a propensity to intervene in the region (whether overtly or by proxy) to 'get things done', because the region is perceived as hostile, irrational, and incapable of reform. In response to this, others have argued for the opposite—they acknowledge the West's bad record in the region, but then propose cutting everyone's losses and leaving. In effect, they're saying: 'We've done so much damage here and it appears we can only make things worse. We messed up so much, that the best we can do is just leave this region alone. Maybe if we leave, everything will get better. Maybe the region will start to heal, and their resentment will subside.'

In our experience, broadly, two kinds of people use this line—those genuinely concerned about causing harm, and those looking for an excuse to disengage (for all sorts of ideological or economic reasons). Our message may resonate more with those in the first group, but we hope we can manage to change the minds of those in the second group as well.

Either way, we understand where the sentiment comes from—especially when, even eighteen years later, we're still suffering the aftershocks of the Iraq War. Western powers have intervened in the region for most of the past two centuries, with colonial powers—especially France and Great Britain—effectively shaping what the region would become, down to literally drawing borders, and seeding many of its current conflicts and contradictions. In the past fifty years, the United States has replaced the old colonial powers as the heaviest meddler in the region, only compounding the problems and invigorating anti-Western sentiments. We understand that an acknowledgement of this history can lead to a resigned pessimism about what positive role, if any, the West could play.

But simply 'cutting and leaving', after decades of damage, would be tantamount to stabbing a person, then acting like you can undo the damage by pulling out the knife and walking away. It's even worse when you consider the global context—our dictators are hysterical, international norms are no longer respected (or enforced), and other foreign imperial powers such as Putin's Russia are more than willing to fill the vacuum left by retreating Western powers, committing war crimes as they do so. It's not enough to pull the knife out and leave us bleeding. You must become a force for healing.

The 'cut and leave' attitude also underplays the outsized influence that open societies, including Western ones, have—not only in terms of economic and military power, but also with regard to the amount of agency citizens in these countries have. A Western citizen may be entirely cynical about how much they can influence the wider system, but it's important to realise that those who have been born in states that respect their fundamental human rights and give them a chance to participate in shaping their nations' policies are already, on a global level, privileged. This privilege—individual and collective—translates into a moral imperative to help improve the lots of others who are struggling for their fundamental rights.

Finally, while the 'let's cut and leave' line is nowhere near as orientalist as the 'ancient hatreds' line, it still drifts towards the trap of assuming that the West and the Middle East are essentially separate, that what happens 'there' doesn't affect 'here', and that the damage can somehow be contained by simply pulling out. It's also rather pessimistic when it comes to hopes for positive outcomes; it is ultimately a resignation of responsibility, sometimes expressed compassionately ('we don't want to hurt you any more'), and sometimes with frustration and even arrogance ('you'll blame us anyway—we're damned if we do, damned if we don't'). The attitude felt most cruel during the Arab Spring. Some of those pushing it may have been moved to tears by the scenes in the MENA region's squares during the uprisings; do they idolise us only when we inspire them, and then abandon us when the tide turns against us?

No, the region won't heal if the borders are redrawn

'We should have drawn the maps correctly' is a thought expressed with surprising frequency, often with suggestions of 'alternative maps' (it sometimes seems that Western commentators have a fetish for drawing borders and a map of the Middle East at the ready). The thinking behind it often goes: 'We acknowledge that colonial-era borders were unnatural and hastily drawn, so the solution as we see it is to redraw the maps with better borders'. Frustratingly enough, I've even heard this line in meetings with policy makers and parliamentarians.

The colonial-era maps were indeed unnatural and drawn in haste, often with little regard for demographics or even geography—and most importantly, they were drawn by occupying foreign powers without the input of the people of the region. Many in the region continue to see them as symbols not of native autonomy but of Western colonialism. But the deeper and more serious source of resentment is that a region which was historically borderless, allowing fairly free movement of people, goods, and ideas, became divided into multiple states, ruled by feuding dictators.

The European colonialists had exported the nation-state model—a model developed in and for Europe—to a region to which it was alien; a region lacking clear geographical, linguistic, religious, or ethnic borders. The Middle East is a cradle of civilisation, and the absence of major natural borders means that countless ethnicities, tribes, sects, and faiths have intermingled and coexisted there for centuries. The assumption that each 'ethnicity' can be cleanly contained in a particular geographical region is fantasy—the region has always been mixed, and its various components could not be 'divided up' without some serious ethnic cleansing (which unfortunately, and unsurprisingly, followed the importation of the nation-state paradigm).

Imagine if the US, India, and China woke up tomorrow with each of their constituent states or provinces declared independent, instituting their own flags, armies, and currencies, enforcing border controls and visa regimes, and ending the free movement of people and goods. Imagine, further, that each of these constituent states were led by a military dictator. What would be the aftermath of the multiple conflicts that would follow? The drop in GDP? The effect on the production and dissemination of culture? Or most importantly, the resentment of the population—who had no say in this?

It's no shock that the result for the MENA was not successful and prosperous countries, but a mess. And yet some continue with the border-drawing fetish that has created so much resentment. The rise of borders, barriers and imposed separation was a shock to our region, and one we're still suffering from. We aren't angry that colonialists cut up our body the wrong way—we're angry that they cut it up in the first place. It is ironic that Europe, which imposed upon us the concept of the nation-state, today guarantees freedom of movement for people, goods, capital, and ideas. The solution isn't to suggest 'better' borders, but to foster more native agency within existing regions, and more integration among regions.

No, we can't 'just get over it' (even though we'd love to)

Another common line acknowledges the harm caused by nearly two centuries of Western colonialism and neo-colonialism, but— in frustration over feeling blamed for the crimes of long-dead imperialists—throws the ball back into our people's court. 'Yes, it happened, and it was bad; but it happened long before any of us were born, so please stop blaming us for it. Given how long ago it was, you should get over it and help yourselves, and start rebuilding your region.' When French President Emmanuel Macron visited Algeria in late 2017, he used part of his speech to ask its people not to dwell on the past (France occupied Algeria from 1830 to 1962; the war of liberation is within living memory).

We find that there are two kinds of people who indulge in this line of argumentation. Some do not realise the depth of damage caused by Western foreign policy, or the fact that the damage hasn't stopped but continues under various updated guises and rationales. Others acknowledge past damage but are uncomfortable with the suggestion of blame (especially when they feel that they themselves never took part in any imperialism)—and wonder how long the people of the region will stay resentful.

It's difficult for us to 'get over it' when we are threatened, silenced, crushed, imprisoned, tortured, exiled, bombed, maimed, made into refugees, or made to constantly accept another bad option for fear of an even worse one. It's easy to tell us to 'get over it' if you think that what we're talking about is old history—but it's not. Western foreign policy continues to contribute to the maintenance of a terrible and increasingly unstable status quo in the region.

When we talk about grievances, or when we try to place our realities today within historical context, we do not do it for the sake of blame, or to abdicate responsibility over our own destiny, or to encourage people to indulge in resentment and victimhood. We're not saying that we shouldn't help ourselves, or that we shouldn't try to overcome adversity, or that we should remain bitter. Rather, we remember history because it matters and is part of the picture, and understanding it is key to understanding the region's problems, psyche, and possible solutions.

It's not only outright military intervention that kills. You don't have to actually invade or bomb a country to cause damage to its society—you could sell weapons to violent regimes; legitimise them through diplomatic, economic, and cultural means; guarantee them impunity when they commit their crimes; subsidise them through bad policy; or just declare your impotence and turn a blind eye to their crimes. You don't have to actually kill us yourselves—you could just let us die.

It's true, of course, that some amplify grievances into full-blown persecution narratives, which are used to encourage people either to wallow in their victimhood, or to unleash indiscriminate violence at perceived persecutors. But it's one thing for persecution narratives to be attacked from the inside—by native voices—and quite another for them to be attacked from the outside, especially by those who have benefitted from or participated in the persecution. It's the job of native activists to counter these narratives, and to remind those living under dictatorship that, while they do not have as much agency as those living in open societies, their agency is, in the end, all they have.

INTRODUCTION

No, it's not Islam that's the problem

Oh, how many times were we slapped with this line in its various manifestations! Something about us being Muslims seems to make it impossible for us to live in modern states marked by participatory decision-making and respect for basic human rights. Some versions of this argument consider democracy and human rights to be 'Western culture', while others insist that we won't get rid of dictatorship until we become 'more secular'.

To rub it in our face, those peddling this line sometimes point to a world map and mockingly ask, 'Out of fifty-seven Muslim-majority countries, show me a Muslim democracy!' We often answer that, while it's true that most Muslim-majority countries are suffering under dictatorship, it's also true that only a century ago, all but two Muslim-majority nations were occupied by a Western power; this isn't entirely a coincidence. But this response doesn't get to the bottom of it—after all, other previously colonised regions such as Latin America, Southeast Asia, and Sub-Saharan Africa have many democracies.

But this region-by-region breakdown actually gets us closer to the source of the problem—it appears that dictatorship is more a Middle Eastern problem than a Muslim problem, and that the further a Muslim country is from the Middle East, the more likely it is to have a functioning democracy, regardless of its cultural makeup. The largest Muslim-majority country in the world by population is Indonesia—classified as a 'flawed democracy' in 2016 by the Economist Intelligence Unit, but still with a Democracy Index score above Poland, Croatia, and Hungary. It also happens to be the farthest Muslim nation from the Middle East. Why is this? What is it about the Middle East that makes it particularly stubborn to democratisation?

Dr Eva Bellin of Brandeis University has spent decades examining this question. 'Robustness of authoritarianism' in the

Middle East, she posits, is greatly facilitated by Western powers propping up dictatorial regimes because they need them for geopolitical reasons, energy supply, or counterterrorism. Middle Eastern dictatorships have benefitted from military alliances, the sale of advanced weapons, diplomatic legitimisation, economic support, or simply the West turning a blind eye to their terrible human rights record, so long as they are 'cooperative' on key security or economic matters.

Nor does secularisation necessarily lead to democracy (or liberalism). Separation of powers is indeed necessary for functioning democracies—but secularism on its own isn't a panacea or a recipe for enlightenment. The regimes of Stalin, Mao, and Pol Pot were nominally secular, as was the regime of Tunisian dictator Ben Ali, and so is that of the Assads. Their secularism didn't stop them from presiding over brutal police states and suffocating dictatorships; it wasn't about separation of the religious and ruling establishments, but about total control by the ruling establishment of the religious establishment.

Democracy is, in the end, a power-sharing arrangement more than an ideology; it gets a fighting chance when none of the parties in a certain country can overpower the others, and it takes root when this power-sharing goes from being a strategic compromise to a political culture. But when one of the parties in a society is constantly propped up by external powers, allowing it to always overpower all other currents in that society, democracy becomes very difficult to come by. Instead, existing regimes are then able to tighten their grip and eliminate, coopt, or preempt opposition.

No, it's not that 'we're 'not ready for democracy'

It all eventually boils down to this, the line that's often the net result of all of the above. In the words of Dr H. A. Hellyer:

We've seen that from rulers and officials from within the region, of course. To defend, excuse and minimise the seriousness of abuses they oversee or have responsibility for, they revert to this crude style of orientalism. They caricature their own people, so that their own problematic rule is justified. 'Yes, we're abusing our own people— and so what? This isn't the West, and they're not Westerners. We're in a rough neighborhood, we're not all educated, and you need to understand what we are going through—the responsibilities we have—the challenges and problems we face—so leave us be.'[3]

The 'not ready for democracy' line is essentially the same line employed by colonialists in the twentieth century who argued that their subjects were 'not ready for self-rule'—what is democracy, after all, but self-rule? At the time, the Westerners doing the colonising enjoyed democratic rights at home, while systematically denying them to the natives they subjugated. 'They're not ready for self-rule' was a convenient excuse to justify this glaringly unconscionable contradiction. But let's not mince words: To argue that the people of a certain region should be denied democratic rights because they're not worthy of the right to vote is overtly and unabashedly racist—especially when those peddling this line are getting rich off our subjugation.

It is even more obviously racist when you consider that the very reasons cited to justify why we're 'not ready' can easily be applied to Western nations themselves. Was the United States 'ready' for democracy when it started its political experience with the enslavement of one people and the ethnic cleansing of another? Did the US election of a deeply corrupt, authoritarian figure such as Donald Trump prove Americans to be 'not ready' for democracy? Was Europe 'ready' when it destroyed itself—and much of the rest of the world—in two destructive 'World Wars'? Does the spread of bigoted right-wing populism across Europe prove that Europeans are 'not ready' for democracy?

THE MIDDLE EAST CRISIS FACTORY

Charting a Path Forward

Had we written this book in another decade, we'd have had to add another trope to the above list: 'Tyrants are good for stability.' Hopefully, that idea is already obsolete, with many said stable tyrannies causing massive instability. In fact, the Middle East's problems are inextricable from the fact that it is dominated by dictators looking to preserve their own narrow interests, with no regard for the true interests of their societies.

It's about time we realised that dictatorships are not responsible global partners and, if given space, will only create more instability. Whatever appears as 'stability' under a dictatorship is a façade, and even the most formidable dictatorships are always just a few missteps away from crisis. Even worse, because dictatorships hollow out society, eating at it from the inside, they make it brittle and unequipped to deal with any crisis, ensuring absolute chaos when they leave.

For decades, however, many Western powers have harboured the illusion that 'dictators guarantee stability'—and we are living the consequences. This delusional notion is actually one of the deepest causal factors of both dictatorship and instability in our world today.

The cost is already too high—and not only in financial terms, should we tabulate everything spent on counterterrorism, refugee relief, foreign aid, and boosting military defences. There is also an enormous human cost. The MENA's population exceeds 500 million: that's half a billion human beings living under regimes that are not only authoritarian, but—as we'll see in coming chapters—also unsustainable. Half a billion souls, trying to make the best out of life in a region riddled with collapsing paradigms and broken social contracts.

The breakage of a single Middle Eastern country—Syria—has already created an unprecedented global crisis that gave rise to

ISIS, brought on foreign intervention, and created a massive humanitarian catastrophe and millions of refugees. In a world that is more interconnected than ever, fires do not remain contained—they spread. Syria's collapse has arguably directly helped to fuel the rise of populists in the West, who campaigned based on fear-based narratives, warning of Middle Eastern terrorists and Middle Eastern refugees. And that was the breakage of just one country—imagine if the collapse doesn't stop there. It's a problem too big to be managed.

Is there a way out of this spiral? The world seems very willing to discuss such global problems as climate change, extreme poverty, war, refugees, and terrorism—but there's another global problem that dwarfs all of these combined, and it is very often a causal factor in all of them—dictatorship. 52 per cent of the world's population today lives under dictatorships, and yet there is no concerted effort at a global level to tackle it as a problem.

Current foreign policy thinking seems limited in its options for dealing with dictatorship; courses of action range from the legitimisation of dictatorships, in the hope that engagement will bring 'regime moderation', to military intervention, or blanket sanctions, in the hope that the dictators will be coerced into cooperating. Neither of these approaches has brought success, and there is a need for new thinking.

But it gets worse. The West's inability to deal with dictatorships makes it appear hypocritical about its own values, as happens when you claim to venerate democracy, free speech, and human rights but have a foreign policy approach that completely disregards them. A focus on short-term expediency with no long-term strategic vision leads to self-defeating policies and contradictory alliances that antagonise friends and give ammunition to enemies, all while increasing mistrust and cynicism towards the West in the Middle East and the world.

THE MIDDLE EAST CRISIS FACTORY

Our region is today a 'crisis factory'—but it was once a shining light unto the world, a centre of enlightenment, art, and culture. The cost of instability shouldn't only be assessed in finances or security budgets, but also, importantly, in stunted human potential. A region that once contributed so positively to humanity—and that has very recently inspired the world with scenes of bravery and hope—is today stuck in a spiral of violence and despair.

We have written *The Middle East Crisis Factory* to help readers to understand the power structures and interdependent narratives that are creating that very spiral, and to present some ideas about how to undermine dictatorships without causing societal collapse and without resorting to overt military intervention. The book grew out of our frustrations and fears, but also our hopes. A central assumption of the book is that you—the reader—care, and that you realise that we're not truly free until we're all free, and we're not truly safe until we're all safe.

PART I

HISTORY

1

BROKEN PROMISES

The number of democracies in the world increased on every inhabited continent through the twentieth century. The total went from twenty-four in 1948 to seventy-five in 1993, peaking at eighty-five in 2005.[1] The MENA region was uniquely excepted from this 'wave of democratisation', though, being the only part of the world in which no progress was made.[2] Today, only one Arab country is classified as a full democracy, Tunisia.[3] At the same time, as of late 2020, our region has lived through four civil wars, four proxy wars, three refugee crises, and four major terror flashpoints—as well as nine major popular protest movements—since 2018.

In 2019, as a new wave of uprisings shook the region, a video clip of a Moroccan football chant went viral. In unison, thousands of young people in a stadium in Casablanca sung these painful verses:

In this country, we live in grief
All we seek is to be safe
Our talents, you waste
Our dreams, you break

Our country's wealth, you steal
Our generation, you crush
Our passion, you kill
And now you provoke us?
You pass laws against violence
But by violence want to rule us?[4]

There is a reason why the clip was so popular: it could have been sung in any city in the MENA. Our region lives in the midst of a protracted legitimacy crisis that has surpassed the political and seeped into its social, cultural, and religious spheres. The origin of uprising is not mobilisation—that comes rather late in the process. Rather, the origin of uprising is a broken social contract. Dictators do not rule by force alone—they also rule by fraud, threats, and promises, until they run out of lies.

Social contracts are fundamental promises made by the leaders of the political order, upon which their legitimacy is based. Most histories of our region focus on political actors or conflict; this may inform you of all the wars and who won them, but it will leave you with rather little understanding of how the people of the region felt about these events. Here, we will put societies at the centre, narrating our modern history as a series of social contracts, through to their breakage.[5] We believe that our history of resistance and resilience can only be understood through this prism.

Origins of a Political Order

Between the eighth and thirteenth centuries, the Middle East's societies were among the world's most advanced. Polymaths and innovators in mathematics, astronomy, physics, chemistry, engineering, arts, and philosophy produced lasting contributions to human knowledge, laying the groundwork for, among other things, Europe's later renaissance. Diverse people from the region's many ethnicities and faiths contributed to this Golden Age.

But all good things come to an end, golden ages included. The political order would be devastated by the Crusades in the twelfth century, the Mongol invasions in the thirteenth century, and the Black Plague in the fourteenth century—and it never fully recovered from these blows. The region slipped into a centuries-long period of decline, despite the rise of a new power— the Ottoman Empire—which consolidated control over much of the Middle East. The Ottomans were rightfully considered a world power, but in the ensuing centuries the Middle East was no longer the global centre of culture, enlightenment, and economic dynamism that it once had been.

The legitimacy of the political order continued to lean upon religion, and it was rarely successfully challenged. Contact between communities across the region continued, thanks to long-established trade routes and yearly religious pilgrimages— but contact with the West was limited, even as Europe underwent a Renaissance and an Enlightenment.

In the aftermath of the French Revolution and as part of the ensuing Revolutionary Wars, Napoleon's army invaded Egypt in 1798 in an attempt to secure French trade interests and undermine Britain's access to its Indian colony. The French occupation of Egypt would last for only three years, but it was a harbinger of what was to come. The Ottoman Empire was past its own Golden Age—and its reformist and constitutionalist movements which emerged in the eighteenth and nineteenth centuries were too late in the face of greater forces that had been set into motion.

Exploiting Ottoman decline, France would invade the Maghreb (Algeria, Morocco and Tunisia) in the nineteenth century. The British invaded Egypt in 1882, having already expanded their influence over the Arabian side of the Gulf, all the way to the Iraqi port of Basra. Italy, for its part, invaded and occupied Libya in 1911. After the Ottoman Empire was defeated in World War One, the French and British divided the Levant region between them. France took Syria and Lebanon, whilst the British took Iraq, Jordan and Palestine. New borders were drawn in the infamous Sykes–Picot agreement, which divided a long-integrated region into new nation-states, importing European systems of governance.

Out of all countries in the modern MENA, only Saudi Arabia, Turkey, and Iran were not completely colonised—although Iran came very close, with both Russian and British influence and intervention lasting well into the twentieth century.

European colonisation was a kind of foreign rule that was markedly different from previous empires that had risen and fallen in the Middle East over millennia. It had a deep impact on the region's political order, indeed on its very psyche. Perhaps most insidious was that it brought new narratives of a 'civilising mission' that called into question whether the natives were even fit to exercise any agency over their political affairs. In that same period, the people of both France and the United Kingdom enjoyed democratic rights at home—a contradiction that could only be explained by resorting to racist tropes of the type explored in the previous chapter.

In fact, colonialism is defined by its inherent racism. More fundamental than its enactment of occupation, subjugation, exploitation, and violence is the idea that no matter what the natives do, they will never be equal to the colonisers. The colonisers justify their subjugation and right to determine our fate not merely because they are more powerful than us, but because they are better than us. We may try to assimilate, to literally become similar to the colonisers; while that might make us a little bit more human-like in their eyes, we will never be equals. To acknowledge our full humanity would make them unable to defend their denial of our agency—and how could they, when their prosperity and their status in the world depends upon it? This is the essence of European colonialism, and this is why it was an evil unmatched by that of the other numerous empires that had come and gone.

Colonisation also imported new economic and political systems, including modern capitalism and the nation-state; these brought with them a level of administrative control that did not exist before. The people of the MENA, coming from a region with a proud history, had to contend with a new reality in which they were dominated by foreign nations largely richer, more educated, and freer than they were.

The late colonial period—roughly corresponding to the first half of the twentieth century—kicked off a decades-long soul-searching across the region. Are the colonialists correct when they say we are mere savages, unfit for self-rule? If so, does mimicking the colonialists in the way they speak, dress, and eat make us more 'civilised'? Or is the answer in copying the way they think, trade, administer—even repress? Should we engage with the colonialists to learn more about their new theories and technologies? And if we do, how can we make sure it's an equal exchange, given the enormous disparity in power? Perhaps the colonialists present an opportunity—their superior weapons and their hunger for natural resources could enable interesting alliances; perhaps for the right price, they will assist us against our enemies?

Or maybe the colonialists are wrong, so wrong that we should do the opposite of everything they do, reverting instead to our traditional systems of knowledge. Should we isolate ourselves from the colonialists as much as possible, even if it means pushing away all the material success and scientific knowledge that they boast? These questions were asked by generation after generation, leading to a new ecosystem of ideologies and political movements representing every side of each question.

Virtually every society across the region saw an anti-colonial struggle for independence and self-determination, but it was in the mid-twentieth century that the European colonial powers, exhausted by World War Two, would withdraw from much of the region, giving rise to a new political order in freshly independent states.

Perhaps now, the people of the region thought, was the time for native agency.

We will not return to chains
We have become free and liberated the homeland!

from the Libyan national anthem, 1951[6]

1950s–1970s: 'We Liberate You—And You Shut Up'

In the decades following World War Two, European nations withdrew from their colonies, unable to afford to maintain them and exhausted from constantly having to suppress native liberation movements. In 1946, Syria and Lebanon became independent from France, and Jordan from Britain. Egypt had gained its independence from Britain in 1936, although Britain maintained control over the Suez Canal until 1956. Libya gained its independence in 1951, after a period of UN stewardship. Five years later, in 1956, Tunisia and Morocco became independent from France; Sudan gained its independence from Britain in the same year. In 1961, the British protectorate over Kuwait ended, making it an independent state. In 1962, Algeria gained independence from France, after a brutal war of over seven years that according to some estimates cost over a million lives.[7] Yemen became independent in 1967, and the Gulf states in 1970 and 1971.

Even in Saudi Arabia, which was never colonised, Western powers were instrumental to the rise of the modern state. In 1915, the British signed the treaty of Darin with Emir Ibn Saud—the ruler of Najd (central Arabia), who had fought the

Ottomans—making his lands a British protectorate and giving him military support. The treaty of Jeddah in 1927 gave diplomatic recognition to what was to become the Kingdom of Saudi Arabia five years later. In return, Britain expected Ibn Saud to stop the religious extremists that he commanded from attacking neighbouring states within their sphere of influence.

In many countries in the region, the modern nation-state was not just new but alien to lived realities. The ideal nation-state consisted of a fairly homogeneous nation that spoke one language and lived within well-defined historical borders. How does this apply to a region in which many indigenous groups speaking numerous languages have coexisted for millennia—one which was largely borderless, allowing people to trade and move freely? Even though the model was ill-fitted for the MENA, given that the most powerful countries in the world were nation-states, a question arose: If we adopted their model, would we achieve the same level of power, prestige, and dignity?

Across the region, a new class of leaders emerged who derived their legitimacy from the struggle for self-determination. Tunisia was ruled by Habib Bourguiba, who had led the struggle for independence and spent over twenty years in French prisons. In Algeria, Ahmed Ben Bella—one of the leaders of the anti-colonial National Liberation Front (FLN)—took power, before being overthrown by his own defence minister after two years.

This was happening in a global context in which rivalry between Western countries and the Soviet Bloc was evolving into a Cold War. Given that the region's most prolific colonialists, the United Kingdom and France, were both part of the Western Bloc, many political movements in the MENA sought to align themselves in opposition to their previous colonialists.

In many newly established states, post-independence governments perceived to be weak or beholden to the previous colonialists were overthrown in military coups. In Syria, the military overthrew the civilian government in 1949; military coups also toppled monarchies and civilian governments in Egypt (1952), Iraq (1958), and Libya (1969).

These were anti-Western coups, but there were coups in the opposite direction too; most famously the 1953 CIA-assisted coup against Iran's democratically elected Prime Minister Mohammad Mosaddegh. The coup enabled Iran's monarch, Mohammad Reza Pahlavi, to centralise his rule; Iran would remain closely allied with the Western Bloc—and highly author-itarian—until the 1979 revolution overthrew the monarchy, bringing to power an intensely anti-Western and equally authori-tarian theocratic regime.

In general, the region's post-independence rulers built highly centralised, autocratic states that, ironically enough, borrowed a lot of their repression strategies from the previous colonial-ists. Colonel Adib al-Shishakli, architect of the 1949 coup in Syria, presents a notable case study, and would be a harbinger of what was to come. He abolished political parties, setting up a one-party state led by his staunchly nationalist 'Arab Liberation Movement'. He established a cult of personality, which he amplified by expanding the state-supervised media, making his face ubiquitous in public life. This control of the media allowed him to valorise and expand the armed forces, police, and security services, and invent and exaggerate threats against the state. Being a veteran of the French mandate-era gendarmerie, he was already experienced in using security forces to control the population.[8]

Shishakli was deeply inimical towards religious institutions, banning religious clothing, curtailing religious education, and ensuring that all religious establishments became organs of state. At the same time, he was intensely suspicious of ethnic and reli-gious minorities, and in the legacy of colonial 'divide and rule' tactics, he pursued a strategy to marginalise them. He shut down their institutions, limited their use of minority languages, and forbade the usage of 'foreign' names. Ironically, he was himself of Syrian Kurdish descent.

Shishakli even staged national elections in 1953, in which he (of course) won 99.7 per cent of the vote. Ultimately, Shishakli was only in power until 1954, but the methods he pioneered were picked up by Gamal Abdel Nasser in Egypt, Saddam Hussein in Iraq, and Muammar Gaddafi in Libya, as well as by his future successor Hafez al-Assad.

By now, the division of the Arab world into nation-states had given rise to a backlash. After generations under colonialism, many people across the region faced a crisis of identity that led them to prioritise identitarian narratives over political freedom; this brought on the heyday of Arab Nationalism. One anecdote exemplifies this. Algeria's Ben Bella was invited to give a speech in Egypt at the behest of Nasser, then considered to be the foremost leader of Arab Nationalism. Ben Bella started to speak, but then burst into tears at his inability to communicate in standard formal Arabic, having lived his entire life speaking French instead. '*Nous sommes Arabes, nous sommes Arabes, nous sommes Arabes!*' he passionately declared in a speech following independence.

Arab Nationalists sought to erase the borders entirely and unite into a single state;[9] the years between 1958 and 1972 saw multiple attempts at Arab unification, such as those between Egypt and Syria (1958–61) and Iraq and Jordan (1958). There were also talks about the unification of Egypt and Iraq; Egypt and North Yemen; Egypt, Syria, and Iraq; and Egypt, Syria, and Libya—none of which ever came about. Each of these states were led by leaders with their own cults of personality, who clashed with each other constantly.

Among the greatest sins of the Arab Nationalism movement was that it suppressed the region's native ethnic minorities, forcing a single prevailing identity. The Middle East's Kurds and

Assyrians and North Africa's Amazigh were among its most notable targets. In effect, Arab Nationalism adopted the colonial concept of the ethnic nation-state, applying it to Arabness writ large. A deeply pluralistic region, one that for all of its history was composed of multiple layered identities, was forced to acquire a homogenous singular identity; dissenters were immediately accused of being a colonial 'fifth column'. (When Islamism was in the ascendant after the failure of Arab Nationalism, it continued with the same sin—only replacing an ethnic identity with a religious one; Islamism may frequently use the language of theology, but at its heart it is in fact a nationalistic ideology.)

All of this was done, of course, in the name of independence, native agency, and the struggle against colonialism. The nationalist leaders got very good at using the struggle against Western imperialism to silence dissent and control political life. The highly centralised, security-minded Arab Nationalist states were one-party military dictatorships that skilfully used constant internal and external threats—and the romantic dreams of regional unity and revival—as key elements of their social contract. Meanwhile, political life was stunted, dissenters were ostracised and often purged, minorities were suppressed, and the economy was further centralised in the name of sovereignty, under the banner of nationalisation.

The heyday of Arab Nationalism wouldn't last; in 1967, the combined armies of Egypt, Syria, Jordan, and Iraq were dealt a crushing defeat by Israel. But confidence in the Arab Nationalist cause was destroyed by its leaders' own hubris—Nasser's Arab Nationalist radio station had broadcast updates assuring listeners that the offensive against Israel had been a roaring success, and that Arab armies had penetrated as far as Tel Aviv, when in fact the offensive had collapsed and Israel's tanks had reached the Suez Canal. 'Alternative facts' are nothing new to the region, though they were harder to debunk before the internet. When the truth came out, the sense of humiliation was palpable. Across the Arab world, people were so anguished that there was wailing in the streets. Today, the 1967 war is referred to in Arabic-speaking countries as the *Naksa*—the failure. Nasser would continue to lead Egypt until his death in 1970, but the cause of Arab Nationalism never recovered.

Although many Arab states would continue to appeal to anti-imperialism and Arab Nationalism, the post-colonial heyday of 'the struggle' as the basis for the social contract was over. These satirical verses by Egyptian poet Ahmed Foaud Negm perhaps capture the breakage of this social contract:

> *No voice is above the sound of the battlefield!*
> *Everybody has to assist the battlefield*
> *You don't exist if you don't exist for the battlefield*
> *Our bread is black because... for the battlefield*
> *Our people are hungry... it's for the battlefield*
> *Shut up boy and chant... long live the battlefield*
> *But where is the battlefield?*
> *Police! Hunt that scoundrel, that spy!*
> *Chant, boy, no voice is above*
> *The sound of the battlefield.*[10]

The verses were composed in the 1970s, in the Sadat era; the usage of the battlefield to shut down all political dissent had been a fact for decades by then, but it had suddenly stopped working. A new social contract was needed if these unelected regimes were to maintain legitimacy.

In a late post-mortem, prominent Egyptian-American scientist Farouk El-Baz wrote a reflection in 2006 on the 1950s and 1960s, recalling the mood in the higher education institutions of the Arabic-speaking world in that era.[11] He described the limitless aspirations of a region catching up with the rest of the world, combined with the boundless energy of young people who knew they were the best their countries had to offer. 'The future was in our hands,' he wrote, 'and we had four ambitions in which we would not even contemplate the possibility of failure.' They were Arab unity; liberation of Palestine; achieving social justice; and ending illiteracy.

We have seen how those decades saw the pursuit of the first two projects end in dismal failures—now let's see what transpired with the other two aspirations.

1970s–1990s: 'We Give You Jobs and Education—And You Shut Up'

Starting from the 1970s, the region's social contracts began to shift, from a legitimacy that leaned heavily on grand nationalist visions, to one based mainly upon economic welfare. The failure of Arab Nationalism was a major reason for this shift, but there were other important factors as well. A series of economic measures undertaken by the United States in the early 1970s (sometimes referred to as the 'Nixon shock'), culminating with the 1973 oil crisis, created an international financial system that saw billions of dollars flow to oil-rich states. Most countries in the Middle East had exploitable oil and gas reserves. The newfound wealth allowed the funding of ambitious plans to provide economic opportunities, education, and social services to the masses.

Soon, the legitimacy of governments in the population's eyes became inextricably tied to their ability to provide and develop services, particularly health and education. When European colonialists left in the mid-twentieth century, literacy rates in the region were very low, despite the 'civilising mission' of the former (when the French left Algeria after 132 years of occupation, the literacy rate stood at less than 15 per cent).[12] The situation did not improve dramatically over the next few decades—by the 1970s, only about 27 per cent of Arabs aged fifteen and above could read and write.[13]

But now that their legitimacy depended upon it, governments confronted poor education and health services with a new vigour. New wealth from natural resources allowed new schools and hospitals to be built, and in several countries universal education was implemented. Life expectancy rose, and infant mortality fell, leading to a baby boom.

On the economic front, obsession with self-sufficiency and suspicion of the West had led to a focus on state management of the economy and centralised planning. During the Cold War, much of the region swung towards the Eastern Bloc, running highly centralised command economies. Eventually, development slowed and economic stagnation ensued, with the rise in quality of life faltering. The windfall in the aftermath of the 1973 oil crisis was a double-edged sword. Many Middle Eastern states had sizeable oil reserves, and oil income greatly aided their budgets, making several countries fabulously rich. But oil income also meant that many an Arab regime did not need to consider economic sustainability at all; they could follow economically counterproductive policies if doing so might ensure their own survival.

Not all of the region's regimes abandoned the grand anti-imperialist visions that had already crashed. For example, the regimes of Gaddafi in Libya, Saddam in Iraq, and Assad in Syria continued to appeal to these slogans even as they implemented ambitious social welfare plans; after 1979 in Iran, a new Khomeinist regime appealed to revolutionary pan-Islamism. Unfortunately, having two legs to stand on only meant that these regimes could repress their people even more, while gaining prestige among some holdover intellectuals who prioritised anti-imperialism over political freedom.

The doors to political involvement of the citizenry remained shut. Gradually, we went from regimes that ran their countries like the former colonists to regimes that ran their countries like new capitalists—as private property. This accelerated after the fall of the Soviet Union and the rise of US-led globalisation, which saw several Arab regimes embrace the new world order, seeking a relationship of clientelism that could strengthen their grip on power. Meanwhile, a newly created middle class was enjoying new economic opportunities and prioritised these over pressing for political reforms, such as separation of powers, free speech, and representative institutions.

The result for us was, again, autocrats who behaved with impunity and eliminated anyone who dared dissent. Leaders who assumed power in the 1980s on average ruled longer than their predecessors, giving rise to multi-decade presidents. Even in countries that were nominally electoral republics, there were no term limits and election results were always known well before the election. In Tunisia, Bourguiba was declared president for life in 1975. In Egypt, Hosni Mubarak ran unopposed in 1981, 1987, 1993, and 1999; in Syria, Hafez al-Assad ran unopposed in 1978, 1985, 1991, and 1999.

But while these decades were marked by domestic political stagnation, regimes that now derived their legitimacy from their ability to provide jobs, education, and health care had to do just that. It was an era of demographic maturation and social and economic progress. Over three decades, the region urbanised and industrialised, changing old economic and social structures. Workers in traditional peasant or manual labourer families began to have office careers, and incomes began to rise. As large segments of the population became literate for the first time and a new generation of young people began to attend college, the structure of society started to change deeply.

The region's average Human Development Index shows an increase of 50 per cent across the Arab world between 1980 and 2010—double the global average rate of increase.[14] In Egypt the increase was as high as 59 per cent.[15] Youth literacy—a subject we'll return to—is today above 90 per cent in most Arab countries, and virtually 100 per cent in Saudi Arabia, Libya and Kuwait.[16]

But a social contract based on the elimination of poverty and illiteracy could only last for so long—once these goals were achieved, they were taken as a given, and a new generation expected more. This is a well-documented phenomenon; as American academic Samuel Huntington observed in his book *Political Order in Changing Societies*, economic development breeds social mobilisation: changes in the aspirations of individuals, groups, and societies.[17] Crucially, he also observed that when the demands of social mobilisation for participation exceed the capacity of existing institutions to accommodate them, political order breaks down.

A new generation grew up far removed from both their grandparents' struggle for independence and their parents' struggle against illiteracy and extreme poverty. Furthermore, the explosion of satellite TV in the 1990s brought independent global news coverage to the region, and the advent of the internet soon afterwards would make the MENA far more connected, both internally and with the rest of most world. That only raised the bar of aspirations of the region's youth, who found themselves crammed against the low ceiling of what the regimes could or would allow.

A new generation came of age that was more literate, more prosperous, more connected, with greater access to a diversity of opinions and worldviews than any generation that had preceded it. Although this younger generation was raised with the same suspicion of Western imperialism as their parents, in their lived experience, their own governments were equally untrustworthy. This distrust was shaped not only by the disillusionment of their parents, but also by the failure of the governments to deliver the dignified life to which they aspired. Yet, despite this loss of trust, as societies matured, there was little or no attempt by the

regimes to create inclusive or democratic states. The governments clamped down on civil society and prevented the rise of
any alternatives.

Those of us born and raised in the region can remember how
by the end of the twentieth century, there was a general feeling
among many that the entire political order lacked legitimacy, and
that we lacked dignity. These regimes suppressed our voices
under the pretext that they were providing health and education—but these were now considered very low bars. Meanwhile,
our rulers were fabulously rich, surrounded by a newly wealthy
elite, and their authority was so deeply entrenched that there was
no hope of ever shaking them off. Were we doomed to lives of
stagnation, living under a very low ceiling of hopes and dreams?
What were we even being suppressed for now, anyway? Did we
have any hope of living, like other nations do, with dignity in our
own countries, fully expressing our agency?

2000s–2010: 'We Fight Terrorism—And You Shut Up'

Dictators, we remind you, do not rule by force alone. They rule
by both force and fraud, until they run out of lies. By the early
twenty-first century, most of our dictators were already running
short on legitimacy—until the war on terror gave them a new
lease of life.

> For over eighty years our nation has suffered this indignity and this
> humiliation, its sons killed and its sacred things attacked ... a million
> innocent children are murdered in Iraq ... and not a single fatwa
> from the scholars of the sultans![18]

The above lines were part of a televised message by Osama Bin
Laden broadcast a few weeks after the single most spectacular
terror attack in history—11 September 2001. Bin Laden's words
tapped into decades-old grievances, recalled anger about the
denial of self-determination, and connected the daily indignities

and hardships of life to the power politics played by Western governments in the MENA region and wider Muslim world. A reservoir of resentment was now being weaponised by non-state actors who were side-stepping the states and attempting to steal legitimacy away from them.

But the outcome would ultimately be exactly the opposite. The 9/11 terror attacks eventually proved a godsend to tyranny in the Middle East, allowing most regimes to use the threat of terrorism to boost their contested legitimacy and gain direct support from Western governments, particularly the United States, as allies in their 'war on terror'.

To many Americans, the 9/11 attacks seemed to come out of nowhere—but to really understand their origins, we have to go back a few decades. As disillusionment grew after the 1967 *Naksa*, many of the masses in the MENA began to embrace Islamism as an alternative identitarian narrative. The lack of space for political contribution meant that identity was the only vehicle of dissent, and the mosque was the last public space not completely throttled by the state.

The watershed year was 1979. In January, the Shah of Iran fled his country into exile. In April, Iran became an Islamic Republic led by Ayatollah Khomeini, whose theocratic faction managed to hijack a popular revolution against the brutally authoritarian monarchy. The new Iranian regime called for Islamic revolution across the world, making the Saudi ruling establishment, in particular, very anxious.

In November, the Saudi regime faced perhaps the most serious crisis in its modern history, when a group of religious extremists infiltrated and seized the Grand Mosque in Mecca, Islam's single holiest site. Those responsible had long been dismayed by recent modernisation and social changes in the country and claimed that the Saudi state was illegitimate. Although the attackers were ultimately defeated, the Saudi regime knew it faced a crisis of legitimacy.

In December, the Soviet Union's invasion of Afghanistan provided a rare opportunity to regain this legitimacy—by supporting a jihad by Muslim Afghans against the ungodly Soviets, the Saudi regime could present themselves as defenders of Islam. For other Arab regimes, supporting the jihad would redirect a domestic Islamist threat externally. The Saudi monarchy, in collaboration with Egypt, Pakistan, and the United States, would finance and facilitate the recruitment and training of thousands of young Arabs to join the jihad, exporting their most motivated and dangerous citizens. Among the beneficiaries was a young man named Osama Bin Laden, the heir of a Saudi construction conglomerate.

The Afghan jihad would rage throughout the 1980s, and would see the marriage of several Islamist currents, notably the Muslim Brotherhood-inspired Islamism of Egyptian jihadists with the puritanical Salafi Islam of the Saudis, leading to the development and refinement of new hybrid ideologies. By 1989, the USSR would be defeated in Afghanistan—a defeat that foreshadowed its dissolution. Many of the Arab fighters returning from their successful 'jihad' to their home countries were immediately jailed—except in Saudi Arabia, where they were greeted as heroes.

Bin Laden, then in his early thirties, was loyal to the Saudi monarchy and believed Saudi Arabia to be the 'land of monotheism'. But this honeymoon would not last. When Iraq invaded Kuwait in 1990 over grievances related to oil, borders, and wartime loans, Bin Laden initially offered the services of his mujahideen to his country. But King Fahd had already chosen to allow US troops to deploy into Saudi territory, which outraged and further radicalised Bin Laden. How could the 'land of monotheism' choose to allow foreign troops, infidels, to be stationed on sacred land? Bin Laden turned to using his platform to sharply criticise the government's accommodation with the West—leading in 1991 to his banishment from Saudi Arabia.

Bin Laden found a refuge in Sudan, but eventually he became a diplomatic liability, and they too expelled him in 1996. He returned to Afghanistan, and within weeks issued a declaration of jihad to 'expel foreign troops and interests from the Muslim world'. In pursuit of that holy goal, he argued, Americans and their allies were justifiable targets, wherever they were. Terror attacks by jihadists inspired by Bin Laden would escalate over the next few years, culminating in the catastrophe of 9/11 and its aftermath.

Bin Laden's declaration did not find a great deal of grassroots support, but many Muslims were nonetheless sympathetic to his narrative of humiliation and stolen agency, due to their distrust of both their own regimes and the West. Bin Laden subscribed to a Salafi interpretation of Islam, which most Muslims didn't share, but the normalisation of Salafism was set to explode further in the coming years.

By this point, a triangle had already formed connecting the main agents of political conflict in the Middle East: religious extremists, Western powers, and tyrants. Islamist extremists had arrived as contenders for political power, inspired by a religious passion and a reconstructed Islamic identity. They opposed both their own countries' regimes and the West, arguing that the former were brutal despots who were responsible for the region's current state of humiliation, while the latter were the previous colonialists, who had never really left and who continued to back the dictators. Western crusaders, they said, were back in the region, hoping to destroy Islam, exploit the resources, and reclaim the spoils of the colonial era. Governments were puppets—tyrants supported by the bigger tyrant of Western imperialism.

This sense that colonialism never ended—that it merely found local proxies, allowing the West to subjugate us while keeping its hands clean—was not new, nor was it fringe. The region's native

terrorists were relying on more than just popular grievances—
they also tapped into a sense of absolute powerlessness that so
warped some people's senses that it made wanton violence seem
like strength, and indiscriminate murder feel like dignity. This
too is a colonised attitude which centres the colonialists, even in
opposition to them; suicide attacks would become an extreme
example of this, where killing Westerners carried more value
than preserving our own native lives.

Initially, Bin Laden and his Al-Qaeda group had hoped to
inspire a grassroots Islamic revolution in the wider Muslim
world, but they found themselves facing local security forces and
Western intelligence agencies, while lacking allies. It seemed
impossible to overcome their own regimes—the West's support
made them too resilient, and this support only increased with
every terror attack on Middle Eastern soil. In a series of self-
reflective lectures in the late 1990s, jihadist theorist Abu Musab
al-Suri articulated the need for a change of strategy.

Al-Qaeda would now seek to overcome the region's governments by making it too expensive for the West to continue supporting them. They believed that direct attacks on the West
would either force Western governments to reconsider their support for dictators, or would draw them to invade. In al-Suri's
view, foreign invasions could be very helpful, because they would
secure the narrative of a Western crusade against Islam, mobilis-
ing the masses to rise up in jihad. Western governments,
embroiled in insurgencies across the Muslim world, would be
financially drained to exhaustion. Soon they would have no
choice but to retreat and stop supporting our tyrants, at which
point the stage would be set for their fall.

This was the context that led to the 9/11 attacks. 'Why do
they hate us?' America asked, and, ignoring a century of Middle
Eastern history, they reached the conclusion that the hatred was
existential: 'they hate us for our freedoms'. To many a Western
mind, our part of the world did not believe in these freedoms.

For the US, the threat of terrorism now shaped every policy consideration. President George W. Bush declared a 'global war on terrorism', and this became the lens through which all international relations were viewed. The ideals of democracy and human rights could not take priority over security, and though Bush's administration later developed an agenda for supporting democracy abroad, in practice this too amounted only to a PR campaign for the war on terror.

A black-and-white, with-us-or-against-us worldview dominated; anyone who could feasibly assist in the war on terror would be an ally and receive support, regardless of their authoritarianism, and anyone who refused to cooperate was an enemy. 'Every nation, in every region, now has a decision to make. Either you are with us, or you are with the terrorists,' President Bush stated. This echoed Bin Laden's own statement from his earlier speech: 'The world is now divided into two camps—a camp of disbelief, wherein there is no faith; and a camp of faith, wherein there is no disbelief.'[19]

As it happens, the biggest winner out of this new situation was political tyranny in the MENA. Dictators benefitted through increased support from the West in order to 'fight terror'. They benefitted through the reinforcement of narratives that they were the people's protectors against murderous extremists, and from the global renewal of the decades-old pretext of terrorism to silence political dissent. They benefitted when constant tensions in the Gulf region led to a boost in the price of oil, sending more billions into their coffers. They even benefitted from Western narratives about how the masses of the Middle East 'hated us for our freedom' and therefore, of course, could never want freedom for themselves.

And so, a regional order of dictators who had nearly run out of legitimacy were given a new boost. Even Gaddafi, an anti-Western dictator, managed to win Western support by giving up his WMD (weapons of mass destruction) programme and joining the war on terror in exchange for normalisation of US–Libya relations. Meanwhile, the new US-led military campaigns in the region boosted the narratives of the other anti-Western dictators, who pointed to these 'wars of aggression' to argue once again that, in Negm's words, no voice was above the sound of the battlefield, which superseded all other demands.

For most of the regimes, the choice was clear: joining the fight against jihadist terrorism meant good relations with the world's now-only superpower. This could mean US military and financial aid, as well as diplomatic support and shelter from criticism. The regimes remained free to do what they wanted to their own societies, and in their prisons—in fact, they were rewarded for prison brutality, so long as they helped to 'interrogate' terror suspects on behalf of America. The US government, in return, praised many crucial MENA regimes for their success in 'ensuring stability' and for being 'key allies against terrorism'.

The only regime that refused to cooperate with the US 'war on terror' was Saddam Hussein's; within two years, the people of Iraq would suffer the direct consequence of this defiance. For the rest of the regimes of the Arab world, generous 'anti-terror' support—in the shape of military-directed and security funding—became a crucial new pillar of their stability. The strength and survival of the regimes was now even less dependent on negotiating popular buy-in from their citizenry.

It just so happened that the war on terror also greatly benefitted the terrorists—after all, as some of al-Suri's disciples understood, foreign invasion was a good way to ignite a popular jihad. Terror groups proliferated throughout the Iraq War, and their recruitment numbers swelled with each atrocity committed by the US over the next decade. As we will see in the next chapter, the war eventually created enough regional chaos for jihadists to establish a base much closer to home.

BROKEN PROMISES

At this point it becomes important for us to segue from the conversation on social contracts and dive deeper into the dynamic touched upon in the above history. The resilience of authoritarianism in the MENA has been aided greatly by the interplay between these regimes and the external world. To explore this, we need to look at what we call the vicious triangle of tyranny, terrorism, and foreign intervention.

2

THE VICIOUS TRIANGLE

In the previous chapter, we discussed the social contracts—unwritten bargains controlling expectations and behaviour—that govern the relationship between states and societies in the MENA region and how these have changed over the course of six decades. The political order in these years was deeply authoritarian, but implicit in it was a degree of development and social progress. This progress, slow as it may have been, meant that each contract contained the seeds of its own demise, and that each was destined to become redundant as the population outgrew it.

But why did authoritarianism last so long, and how did it become so violent and resistant to challenge? Why did these specific social contracts come about as opposed to others, and why was progress so limited? Another level of analysis helps to explain this, rather than looking only at the relationship between states and citizens.

Post-independence, the MENA saw the emergence of an ecosystem of power that existed in opposition to the aspirations of the masses, centring on controlling them and ruling dominated subjects. This power structure was not only comprised of the tyrants who presided over authoritarian states; it also included foreign governments and violent terrorist movements. In a vicious triangle, these three dominant forces worked in tandem to keep the region's societies crushed, impoverished and immiserated.

The most insidious thing about the triangle is the fact that it is self-reinforcing and self-perpetuating: terrorists, tyrants, and foreign intervention need each other to continue to exist and thrive—a gruesome symbiosis. Tyrants justify their repressive rule in the name of either fighting terrorism or resisting foreign enemies; these existential threats are said to require exceptional measures and suspensions of liberties—paradoxically reproducing the very conditions that invite those threats. Meanwhile, the raison d'être of terrorists is normally to oppose either infidel tyrants or crusading invaders; without the pretext of battling these enemies, they would have no popularity, support, or sympathy. Despite this, terrorist movements end up inviting more foreign intervention or entrenching tyranny, as we'll see. As for foreign expansionists and military hawks, there has never been a greater justification than fighting terror or tackling the evils of dictatorship—even though military conflict also reinforces both. In this chapter, we'll examine case studies for each side of the vicious triangle—how terrorists, tyrants, and foreign intervention mutually support and legitimise each other.

Tyrants and Terrorists

We'll start with tyranny and terrorism. Governments typically prioritise prevention of terrorism, provision of security being among government's most basic functions. But dictatorships are not responsible governments, and rule of law and protection of life are not their highest priorities—ruling is. Thus, terrorists and tyrants can sometimes clash in a way that establishes an interdependency between them. This can happen inadvertently, as a result of incompetence, but it can also happen deliberately, with premeditation and planning.

Here we look at two recent cases. In the first, terrorist organisations hijack a popular campaign to overthrow Bashar al-Assad's repressive regime in Syria, but in doing so they throw his regime a lifeline. In the second, the post-2013 Egyptian regime's campaign to fight terrorism ends up aiding the growth of a lethal terror threat in the country.

Syria's Impossible Revolution

As demonstrations started across the Arab world in early 2011, citizens across Syria, ruled for decades by the brutal Assad family, rose up to demand reform to the oppressive system. Their calls were ignored; instead bloggers were arrested and public gatherings broken up by thugs. In late February, eighteen children from Daraa in southern Syria were arrested and tortured for painting the words 'the people want the fall of the regime' on the walls of their school. Protests grew and spread across the country, and security forces responded with gunfire, creating the cause's first martyrs. Chants shifted from calls for reform to calls for the complete overthrow of the regime. Syrians had found their voice. In response, the regime deployed military units across Syria, opening fire on demonstrations and going from house to house to round up activists and campaigners. They besieged towns, cutting off power, water, and phone lines. Tanks were used against civilians, and snipers took positions on rooftops.

By May 2011, the death toll had surpassed 1,000, with many more thousands injured or detained. Reports emerged of soldiers being summarily executed for refusing to shoot at civilians. In June 2011, a group of Syrian soldiers uploaded videos showing their military IDs and announcing that they were defecting from the army. They declared themselves part of a new body to protect protesters—the Free Syrian Army (FSA)—and began to use Syria's pre-1963 flag to signal their total rejection of the regime. The country drifted towards civil war.

Meanwhile, hundreds of videos of brutalised civilians were uploaded to YouTube. A video of the corpse of Hamza Al-Khateeb showed whip-marked flesh covered with cigarette and electrocution burns, his jaw and both kneecaps smashed, and his genitals cut from his body. He was thirteen years old. Traumatic footage, watched by millions, became fuel for radicalisation and was weaponised by the most extreme terrorist organisations.

Little did we know it at the time, but when Bashar al-Assad referred to his people's revolution, a mere week after it had started, as a 'foreign conspiracy' employing 'terrorists', he wasn't offhandedly issuing distracting propaganda—he was laying out a plan.

Poisoning a Popular Uprising

In 2002, almost a decade before the revolution began, US Under Secretary of State John Bolton issued a speech adding Syria to the list of state sponsors of terror. An alarmed Bashar al-Assad declared that 'Al-Qaeda does not exist', claiming that it was a US invention aimed at justifying the war on terror. In fact, Assad's regime was facilitating the movement of foreign fighters into Iraq. Turning the country into a quagmire for the US was a strategic objective; the more the Americans were mired in a mess across the border, the less likely they were to attack Syria.

In 2009, Iraq's prime minister, Nouri al-Maliki, claimed that 90 per cent of all foreign terrorists entering Iraq did so via Syria, repeatedly accusing the Syrian regime of destabilising Iraq.[1] Since 2003, hundreds of fighters from across the Arab world had flown into Damascus International Airport, where they received discounted visa fees and were sped through passport control. From a dedicated bus terminal, they were ferried to eastern Syria to meet with Al-Qaeda in Iraq (AQI) recruiters, working under the close surveillance of Syrian intelligence, and from there crossed the border into Iraq.[2] The government also encouraged Syrians to join the jihad, and in 2003 Syria's Grand Mufti issued a fatwa legitimating suicide bombing against American forces in Iraq. So blatant was Syrian state support for jihadists that for several months, a jihadist recruitment office was located across the street from the US embassy in Damascus.

In October 2008, US army commandos conducted a raid from Iraq into Syrian territory with Black Hawk helicopters. The Syrian regime loudly protested this as an 'act of terrorist aggression' and even organised a mass rally in Damascus, but despite the public posturing Assad received the message—within a few months, the terror camps and underground transit system were dismantled. Over a thousand fighters were jailed on their return to Syria from Iraq, warehoused in prisons such as Saidnaya, Aleppo and Palmyra. Thus, long before the 2011 uprising, Assad's prisons were already teeming with jihadists, whom ex-prisoners described as practically being the prisons' managers. These were not just fresh recruits—they were hardened veterans, ideologues, and terror entrepreneurs. One day—and that day would come soon—they would be needed.

As demonstrations against Assad spread in 2011, one of the main demands by protesters was the release of political prisoners—the scores of dissidents, civil society activists and bloggers held in jail, in addition to newly arrested protest leaders. In September 2011, security forces arrested twenty-five-year-old protest leader Ghiath Matar—dubbed 'Little Gandhi' for his commitment to non-violence; four days later, his tortured corpse was returned to his family. In November, Syrian-American blogger Razan Ghazzawi was arrested, along with journalist and activist

Yara Bader, and free speech activist Mazen Darwish. Open-source activist Basel Khartabil was arrested in March 2012 and executed in 2015 after a brief military trial.

Assad would soon announce an amnesty for political prisoners, but it was the seasoned jihadists who were released, among them four men in Saidnaya who would become the commanders of Jaysh al-Islam, Suqour al-Sham, Liwa al-Haq and Ahrar al-Sham—the four biggest Islamist fighting groups in the country. Forty-six of the Saidnaya releasees also became leading members of Al-Qaeda's subsidiary Jabhat al-Nusra, according to Major General Fayez Dwairi, a former Jordanian intelligence officer.

Nabeel Dendal, former director of political intelligence in Latakia, said he twice led security forces in raids on Al-Qaeda cells, only to learn that the cell leaders were supported by Syrian intelligence. 'The reason the regime released them at the beginning of the Syrian revolution was to complete the militarisation of the uprising,' explained Mahmud al-Naser, an intelligence officer who defected in late 2012, 'to spur criminal acts so that revolution would become a criminal case and give the impression that the regime is fighting terrorists.'[3]

The released jihadists got to work. In December 2011, the battalion called Ahrar al-Sham was declared in Idlib governorate, and shortly after, another group called Liwa al-Islam appeared in the Syrian south.

From Popular Uprising to Jihadist Disneyland

In January 2012, Jabhat al-Nusra was announced. Unlike other fighting groups, this jihadist organisation was intensely ideological from the start, and it actively sought and accepted foreign fighters. It never flew the Syrian revolution's flag—only black-and-white Islamist banners. Other rebel groups initially viewed them with suspicion and even jealousy—they were far better equipped and organised than the defector-based Free Syrian Army, and developed a reputation for bravery that led many to view them as an effective force against Assad, despite their extremist ideology. In April 2013, Jabhat al-Nusra publicly pledged allegiance to Ayman al-Zawahiri, the leader of Al-Qaeda, officially becoming its subsidiary in Syria. A clash of visions ensued within the group, after which a group that called itself the Islamic State of Iraq and Syria (ISIS) split off, with tensions growing between the new group and the other rebel factions.

According to Mahmud al-Naser, Syrian intelligence services watched on in spring 2012 as hundreds of militants crossed the Iraqi border into Syria, following explicit instructions not to touch them. At the same time, Assad continued to let jihadists out of prison. In 2013 his regime exchanged prisoners with Ahrar al-Sham—among those released then were Al-Qaeda recruiter Mohammad Hayder al-Zammar, who joined ISIS and arrived in Raqqa within a matter of days, and Abu Ali al-Shar'i, who also travelled to Raqqa and went on to become a senior ISIS judge.

Meanwhile, Syrians repeatedly called upon Western leaders to decisively arm the Free Syrian Army against both Assad and extremists, or to implement a no-fly zone to neutralise Assad's most devastating weapon, his air force. Yet throughout 2011 and 2012, the US supplied only non-lethal aid to a limited number of FSA groups. Two years into the civil war, with the Assad regime apparently teetering, the CIA finally began a formal 'train and arm' programme for vetted FSA groups, but even this did not see the delivery of anti-aircraft weapons. Many became convinced that the US was prolonging the conflict, thus allowing it to swing towards better-armed Islamist brigades, whilst Gulf monarchies poured fuel on the fire, funding competing groups and running guns to Islamist factions.

In July and August 2013, a coup in Egypt and subsequent massacres seemed to suggest to some that Muslim Arabs would never be allowed to express their agency through democracy. But the worst was yet to come: On 21 August, Assad used sarin-filled rockets against two rebel-held suburbs in Ghouta, near Damascus. Up to 1,729 people were killed within hours. Obama had declared the usage of chemical weapons to be a 'red line', but after the Ghouta massacre, not only did he fail to act upon his own forewarning; he accepted a Russian offer to act as guarantor of the Assad regime's disarmament of chemical weapons. From this point, Russia became a major player in Syria, and Assad would commit dozens more chemical weapons attacks.

The longer the conflict went on, the more radicalised it became. Extremist groups expanded and consolidated by absorbing smaller groups and militias, and by late 2013 the military opposition was unambiguously dominated by Islamists. Groups like Jabhat al-Nusra and Jaysh al-Islam attacked journalists and civil society activists and persecuted religious minorities, destroying shrines, conducting mass killings, forcing Druze civilians to renounce their religion, and carrying out abductions of Alawites and Christian nuns.

This was not inevitable. In 2011 and 2012, before the militarisation of the uprising became complete, Local Coordination Committees organised civilian-led administrations and even local elections across free Syria. Volunteerism flourished and a new sense of agency arose, as citizens started to run their own cities. To prevent a functioning administrative structure from emerging in areas outside his control, Assad adopted a 'scorched earth' policy; opposition-held areas were besieged, starved, and bombed incessantly. Between 2011 and 2016, 454 strikes targeted 310 medical facilities, and more than 4,200 schools were damaged or destroyed. Assad was heeding a lesson the world had learnt from Iraq and Afghanistan—that ungoverned spaces are conducive to the spread of extremist groups.

Civilians were targeted indiscriminately with cluster munitions, barrel bombs, and chemical weapons, as well as sniper attacks, rape, public executions, and mutilation. Nader Hashemi, director of the Center for Middle East Studies at the University of Denver, explained in 2014 that the spread of Islamic radicalism in Syria was 'a direct result of the barbarity of the regime. ... In the midst of the chaos, mayhem, bloodshed and crimes against humanity, you don't produce liberal, democratic opinion. You produce the antithesis of it.'[4]

The population, traumatised through continuous exposure to violence, were also pushed to extremes. Facing the daily risk of being slaughtered, they turned to anyone willing to help. As the conflict wore on and the more moderate groups lost power and influence, this would often mean support for extremists. Assad's effort to make his people's revolution into a binary choice between himself and terrorists was succeeding, and things were only about to get worse. In 2014, Assad's diligent efforts would pay off, and a terror threat far more concrete than the disparate Islamist rebel groups would arise: the caliphate of ISIS.

Assad vs ISIS

As large battles broke out with other rebel factions, ISIS was able to expand its territorial control, capturing Syrian regime military bases with minimal to no resistance. At one point, Palmyra was completely evacuated in advance of an ISIS attack, allowing the militants to capture warehouses of weapons. The group used these pillaged arms to take over the Iraqi city of Mosul, as well as huge portions of Syria and Iraq, including several major oil fields. On 29 June 2014, Abu Bakr al-Baghdadi declared ISIS to be a caliphate, with him as its leader.

The Assad regime signed contracts to buy energy from ISIS and paid it to protect the pipelines passing through its territory. This made Assad the group's biggest funder; documents captured in a raid by US Special Forces reveal that, at the height of production, ISIS oil sales had brought in more than $40 million every month, and revenues in the six months to February 2015 were $289.5 million.[5]

An alliance seemed to be emerging. Defectors from ISIS described being told by their commanders not to intervene as Assad's forces seized towns from more moderate opposition forces. In early 2017, the secretary of the Syrian parliament, Khaled Abboud, told state TV that Syrian intelligence services 'have infiltrated and deeply penetrated [ISIS] ... and taken control of key structures within,' hinting that this was why ISIS attacks had spared Damascus.[6] Later that year, ISIS was able to quietly relocate its forces over several hundred kilometres of regime-controlled territory. Regime aircraft carried out bombings of rebel positions in towns around Aleppo in tandem with an ISIS ground force attack, and Turkish officials revealed having captured radio intercepts of regime forces warning ISIS militants to vacate locations ahead of an imminent bombing campaign. According to Turkey's former prime minister Ahmet Davutoglu, there was a 'behind-the-scenes partnership' between ISIS and Assad's government.

The Russian regime threw its weight behind Assad, declaring its own military operations against ISIS. 'Scorched earth' tactics continued, but by late 2015 it was estimated that less than 10 per cent of Russia's airstrikes were actually against ISIS or Al-Qaeda affiliates—instead, they disproportionately targeted the last remaining FSA strongholds.[7] In September 2017, when ISIS still controlled more than 700 square kilometres in the country, the Russian Defence Ministry proclaimed: 'The Russian forces have achieved their goal of defeating the IS terrorist organisation in Syria.' This prompted no change in the intensity of its airstrikes. Military confrontations between Assad's regime and ISIS were rare—'You would be hard pressed to find many instances of the regime attacking [ISIS],' said Karin von Hippel, a former US

State Department official, 'and the few sporadic attacks that have taken place have targeted more civilians than [ISIS] fighters.'

It's Us or the Terrorists

Once the forces of the 2011 uprisings were defeated, Assad and his foreign sponsors finally turned their attention to ISIS, which eventually crumbled under the combined pressure of Russian-led and US-led attacks. Assad knew he couldn't win against a popular revolution—but he could win a civil war. And if the other side were terrorists, then his own regime's violence was a legitimate 'war on terror', and his survival was all but guaranteed. Assad set out to make the conflict truly binary, by giving Syrians and the world only two choices: 'You are either with us, or with the terrorists.'

The Syrian regime followed a multi-step process to militarise, Islamise, and eventually jihadise the revolution. Assad confronted protests with uncompromising force and radicalising brutality, whilst arresting or eliminating protest leaders, civil society, and all non-violent activists. Whilst clamping down on moderate groups, he released hardened extremists from prison and gave them space to work, through a combination of turning a blind eye, implicit coordination, and direct material support.

The plan worked, and Assad became the least bad choice for much of the international community. Syrian National Council leader Moaz al-Khatib criticised the role of Salafist militants and admitted their prominence had allowed the uprising to be portrayed as extremist. When the revolution began it was lauded internationally; over a hundred nations formed a coalition called 'Friends of Syria' to provide diplomatic support. By 2017 they had all but disbanded and were de-emphasising demands for Assad's resignation.

Regime supporters had repeated, early in 2011, 'Assad, or we burn the country'—and that's exactly what they did. Aided by 'war on terror' precedents set a decade earlier, Assad's cynical efforts to exploit terrorism ensured his regime's survival—but in doing so he broke Syria and worsened the situation in neighbouring Iraq. The second- and third-order effects of this disaster have been enormous, even beyond the tragic human cost; the breakage of Syria directly contributed to the resurgence of populism in the West, as fear of the refugee wave and resurgent terrorists facilitated a wave of authoritarian illiberalism.

Egypt's Revolution Undone

In early 2011, a young Egyptian-American student at Ohio State University called Mohamed Soltan defied his family and booked a ticket on a nearly empty flight to Egypt. He went straight from the airport to Tahrir Square—the main site of the revolution—and didn't leave until the day Mubarak stepped down. 'Right when Mubarak stepped down, people were chanting, "Raise your head up, you're Egyptian." I'd never felt proud of my identity before—I had so much hope for the future, it changed my outlook on life,' says Mohamed.[8]

The Supreme Council of Armed Forces (SCAF)—the leadership of the Egyptian army—took charge of the chaotic year-long transitional period. A deep clash of visions about the future of the country led to mounting polarisation between Islamist parties and non-Islamists, whilst police brutality, military trials of civilians, and other human rights abuses continued. In 2012, the first free presidential elections in modern Egyptian history took place. In a two-round 'first past the post' election—a recipe for polarisation in unconsolidated new democracies—Mohamed Morsi, of the Muslim Brotherhood's Freedom and Justice Party (FJP), narrowly defeated Mubarak's last prime minister.

After the initial euphoria faded, the country was more divided than ever. Opposition to the Muslim Brotherhood culminated on 30 June 2013 in a wave of street protests, in part planned by the military, demanding that Morsi step down. On 3 July, Defence Minister General Abdel Fattah al-Sisi overthrew Morsi in a coup and took power. The next two months were chaotic and violent. The military establishment again took charge, buoyed by a windfall of financial support from the UAE and Saudi Arabia. The death of democracy was not pretty—Sisi suspended the constitution, jailed members of the government (including Morsi himself), dismissed parliament, disbanded the FJP, and criminalised the Muslim Brotherhood. On the morning of 14 August, the Egyptian army committed the largest mass killing in modern Egyptian history, the Rabaa massacre, violently clearing two large anti-coup sit-ins and killing around a thousand civilians in a single morning. We watched as the horror unfolded, aware that when the path to democratic change is shut, the gates of terrorist hell are opened wide.

'Egypt Fights Terrorism'

The successful non-violent revolution of 2011 had demonstrated that achieving change by peaceful means was both possible and far more effective than through violence; Egyptian protesters had achieved in eighteen days what jihadists hadn't over decades of violence. But now, as the coup and crackdowns sounded the death knell of Egyptian democracy, fresh life was breathed into the idea of terrorism.

Extremists gloated that the ideals of democracy and peaceful change had been refuted. In its first statement after the Egyptian coup, ISIS declared, 'And we say to the people of the project of civil state: you have been exposed in Egypt and your idol [democracy] has fallen.' Ayman al-Zawahiri, Bin Laden's successor as leader of Al-Qaeda, released a message reiterating that Muslims could never make gains through the ballot box, and that jihad was the only viable path to political power.

Meanwhile, during the Rabaa massacre by the army, a familiar narrative circulated in Egyptian media: 'Egypt fights terrorism'. Foreign journalists were given press packets bearing the same slogan, which became a round-the-clock staple of every news programme and talk show—at least, the ones still allowed to broadcast. The establishment had learnt over the previous decade that 'the t-word' had a special ability to mute foreign criticism and justify state violence; an exceptional situation demanded exceptional measures.

News stations were taken off air, journalists and activists were jailed, and protesting was criminalised. Thousands of political dissidents were rounded up and sentenced to death or decades in prison; many others were disappeared. Among them was Mohamed Soltan, who was picked up by police officers in his home eleven days after the Rabaa massacre, which he had documented and live-tweeted. Egypt's democratic experiment had come to an end, and the regime became more vengefully repressive than ever.

In May 2014, Abdel Fattah al-Sisi became Egypt's president, winning 97 per cent of the vote in elections that nobody pretended were fair. He used his inaugural speech to promise to defeat terrorism: 'Defeating terrorism and achieving security is the top priority ... there will be no leniency and truce with those who resort to violence.' Before the Rabaa massacre, too, he had asked Egyptians to take to the street to give him 'a mandate to fight terrorism'. War on terror wasn't just a security measure—it was a prime pillar for the legitimacy of a new regime.

The month after the coup saw a massive increase in terrorist violence—while there were 37 reported attacks across Egypt from the start of 2013 up to July, 339 attacks were carried out from July until the end of that year.[9] As time wore on, death tolls mounted. On 5 September, a suicide car bomb exploded near the interior minister's home as he left for work. In December, a bomb targeted a police compound, wounding over 100 officers. Attacks continued throughout 2014, with the largest occurring in July when an attack on a military checkpoint in Egypt's Western Desert region left twenty-two officers dead, and 2015, which saw public prosecutor Hisham Barakat assassinated by a car bomb in Juun. The next month, another bomb carrying 450 kilograms of explosives detonated in front of the Italian consulate.

Terrorists didn't target only state institutions, but also places of worship, particularly Christian churches. A gunman opened fire on a church in Cairo in October 2013, killing four. In December 2016, an explosion at the Church of Saints Peter and Paul in Cairo killed twenty-nine people, and on Palm Sunday in 2017, two further explosions at St. George's Church in Tanta and St. Mark's Cathedral in Alexandria killed forty-seven. The bloodiest attack on a place of worship was on Al-Rawda Mosque in November 2017, when forty gunmen killed 311 people and injured at least 122 during Friday prayers in a village of just over 2,000 people in North Sinai.

As the terror attacks worsened, the state sought even more control over the media—security concerns became a pretext to curtail journalistic freedom. Draconian restrictions were imposed on reporters, and many were jailed. The foreign ministry convened press conferences for foreign reporters, giving them lists of approved words and sources, and Egyptian media outlets were warned not to trust the foreign press. Fines of up to 500,000 Egyptian pounds were introduced in 2015 for journalists who published death tolls that contradicted official army figures (the draft law had originally proposed two-year jail terms but was revised after public outcry).[10] In 2020, Egypt ranked 166th out of 180 countries in Reporters Without Borders' Press Freedom Index.

Meanwhile, the low-intensity insurgency that had raged in Sinai for decades was escalating rapidly. The population here had a history of grievance—the peninsula had been occupied by Israel in the 1967 war, and although it was later returned to Egypt, it remained underdeveloped and neglected, used by both sides as a kind of 'buffer zone'. Wealthy enclaves and resorts were built for tourists and well-off Egyptians, but most of Sinai's natives remained poor and marginalised. The weakening of the security establishment after the 2011 revolution had given militants an opportunity to exploit, and attacks had continued throughout Morsi's term. But it was in the aftermath of the military coup that things had really begun to spiral out of control.

In late 2013, Ansar Bait al-Maqdis, a Salafi-jihadist group that never believed in democracy and considered the Muslim Brotherhood to be apostates, carried out a succession of large-scale attacks. In August, they launched RPGs against two buses carrying security forces in Sinai, killing twenty-four. They also carried out attacks targeting gas pipelines, police compounds and checkpoints, military officers, and intelligence buildings, even succeeding in downing a military helicopter. In late 2014, the group pledged allegiance to ISIS and took on the new name Sinai Province (of the Islamic State). The next year they claimed responsibility for the bombing of a Russian passenger jet which killed 224 people, as well as a wave of simultaneous attacks at more than five checkpoints which killed at least fifty soldiers. All told, terrorists killed over a thousand security personnel in 1,700 attacks across the Sinai peninsula between 2013 and 2017.

The military's response has been equally bloody. After a 2014 attack, Egyptian authorities established a buffer zone in Sinai, expelling 10,000 residents before demolishing their homes. Hours after the Al-Rawda Mosque attack in 2017, Sisi appeared on television to promise 'brute force', and airstrikes were launched against targets in the surrounding areas. A total media blackout was in place in North Sinai for seven months, with journalists unable to investigate or even superficially report on military operations and their methods.[11] Despite this, graphic videos of the army carrying out extrajudicial killings of detainees have emerged.

One resident of the border town of Rafah said: 'I won't lie. I'm more afraid of the army than the jihadists. When you're oppressed, anyone who fights your oppression gets your sympathy.' Another Sinai resident said that after 90 per cent of his village was destroyed in a campaign by security forces, around forty people took up arms.[12] The use of illegal cluster munitions and indiscriminate bombing does not endear the state to anyone. The brutal campaign against terrorism, not only in Sinai but across Egypt and even in Eastern Libya, has itself radicalised people and pushed them towards extremist groups.

Prisons Become Incubators

The Egyptian regime's exploitation of 'fighting terror' to go after its political opponents backfired, and the brutal downfall of democracy gave terrorists an ideological boost. But terrorists also got another important boost—under Sisi's regime, prisons once again became recruitment centres for jihadists.

As an ex-prisoner, Mohamed Soltan attests to this. He was kept on a ward of solitary confinement cells containing people from all political and ideological backgrounds—from veteran leftist activists, to the sons of Muslim Brotherhood leaders, to football fan groups such as the Zamalek Ultras, all the way to members of Al-Qaeda and ISIS. At night, prisoners would communicate through the peepholes of cell doors, giving talks, telling jokes, singing, sharing news—anything to entertain each other. In his eight months on that ward, Mohamed heard plenty of news, and most of it was bad:

> We were hearing that the international community [was continuing] to legitimise and embrace and fund [Sisi], and he's consolidating power, day in, day out. We were in despair, and giving up ... At the

same time, news keeps coming in which the violent camp perceives as victories: events in Iraq and Syria, a new jihadist presence in Libya, the bombing of the Italian consulate in the heart of Cairo, and constant 'expansions'. I would see these guys during recess walking with pride, looking untouchable. Their camp outside was winning. Meanwhile, the pro-democracy folks were deflated.[13]

Mohamed went on hunger strike—the only mechanism of resistance available to him, against both the oppression he was facing and the radicalisation of his fellow inmates. For the last seven months of his imprisonment, he was under individual guard in a separate block and, apart from weekly family visits, was allowed no interactions with anyone but the authorities. With one exception:

> Once a week, one of the ISIS guys was allowed into my cell to try to talk me out of non-violent means of resistance—how it doesn't work, how [the] whole world had abandoned the Arab Spring, and how the only means to effectively change anything is through anarchist violence to flip the system on its head. The whole time I was thinking, why are they allowed in my cell to tell me these things?

There is no way such recruitment attempts could have happened without the authorities turning a blind eye, Mohamed says, not only because of the recruiters' freedom of movement, but also given their access to smartphones with VPNs, allowing them to bypass the state's Internet censorship systems. 'When someone was ready to pledge allegiance [to ISIS], they had messages ready for him. This was more than just them being slick.' Asked whether he thinks the regime has deliberately encouraged radicalisation in order to benefit, Mohamed replies, 'Egypt is a security state. If they were to focus then they could get rid of terrorism, but instead they're focusing their resources on political dissent. Their priority was always dissent.'

At least 60,000 political prisoners have been jailed in Egypt since the coup, with nineteen new prisons built to house them.[14]

They remain in poor conditions, often undergoing physical and psychological torture. The lack of police accountability, due process, or rule of law makes it difficult to ascertain who is or isn't dangerous, and terrorism provides a convenient cover for the state to lock people away. 'Before, whenever the police arrested anyone they accused them of being members of the Muslim Brotherhood,' said Khalid Ali Nour Eldeen, a Cairo attorney. 'After 2014, the fashion became to call them ISIS.'[15] In turn, within prisons the injustice of this repression breeds resentment and despair—the perfect fertiliser for violent ideas. As Mohamed Soltan explains, 'The recruiters don't need to make a compelling argument, because of everything that's around you. All they had to do was make very simple arguments that one must defend [oneself] against repression, with some very basic religious cherry picking as cover.'

Thus Sisi's war on terror predictably ended up facilitating the spread of extremism. The regime used the pretext of terrorism to consolidate its power and hunt political opponents and activists, and the now-energised terror threat spread and entrenched itself while the state's energy was focused elsewhere. The regime's violence and brutality gave recruiters a cause, and its mass incarceration of innocents gave them a fertile environment.

* * *

Tyrants and terrorists, even when they fight, need each other. The cases of Syria and Egypt may be particularly blatant, but the dynamic isn't limited to these examples, or even to the MENA region. The threat of terrorism benefits tyrants on multiple fronts. Domestically, it allows them to shore up their legitimacy by presenting themselves as protectors of the people's security, and also to clamp down on dissenters and civil society activists under the cover of their 'war on terror'. Internationally, it allows regimes to present themselves as responsible partners against the scourge of terrorism, often receiving praise, key security alliances, foreign aid, and advanced weapons.

In turn, tyranny presents the perfect conditions for terrorist groups to recruit and grow by weaponising the grievances of the repressed—agony that is almost impossible to understand without direct experience. The corruption, nepotism, and weak institutionalisation that come with tyranny end up creating a brittle state that collapses unpredictably, leaving nothing behind but an ungovernable power vacuum and a traumatised, often divided society.

In other words, despite their opposition to each other, tyrants and terrorists have a symbiotic relationship: Terrorists need tyrants for recruitment; tyrants need terrorists to justify their power grab. They have more in common than they like to admit: They both do not value human life, engage in massive human rights violations, and suffocate their societies and deny them agency.

'Terrorists vs dictators' is a false choice which has caused immeasurable trauma and anguish. The dichotomy is self-fulfilling, and for decades it has empowered tyrants and terrorists while extinguishing all other alternatives. Part of why it's so insidious is that it is heeded by short-sighted, security-minded policy makers, for whom 'fighting terrorism' is the foreign policy version of 'tough on crime'—a quick soundbite that makes you look tough without requiring much real thought. To participate in this false choice is to legitimise it, and thus to empower the whole conflict to continue.

Now we'll see what happens when a third element is added to the triangle: foreign military occupation.

Tyrants and Foreign Intervention

The presence of tyrants is a blessing for foreign actors who want to intervene to ensure their own gain. In turn, the intervention of self-interested foreign powers, whether military or otherwise, has the net effect of empowering authoritarianism, even if, in the short term, it looks to do the opposite.

One example of this dynamic is Saddam Hussein's rule of Iraq between 1979 and 2003. Despite being motivated by anti-imperialism and hostility towards foreign threats, Saddam's choices over two and a half decades resulted in an Iraq more defenceless and more subject to foreign control than at almost any other point in its modern history. A second example is the approach of foreign powers towards the 2014 Joint Comprehensive Plan of Action, an agreement between the permanent members of the UN Security Council and Iran to relieve sanctions on the latter in exchange for compromises on its nuclear weapons programme. Convinced that war with Iran could be imminent, the Obama administration ushered in a deal that ultimately strengthened the repressive Iranian regime.

Iraq's Indefatigable Militarist

As Saddam Hussein rose to power from 1969, Iraq was developing rapidly. This accelerated in the 1970s, after Saddam nationalised the oil industry and an influx of wealth flowed into social services. Public education expanded, becoming both mandatory and free. Illiteracy was almost wiped out among youth in the 1970s, and Iraq became known for having both the best health care and the best universities in the Arab world, attracting students from across the region.

However, upon formally becoming president in 1979, Saddam almost immediately launched an invasion of Iran. He aimed to quickly occupy the oil-rich provinces, as well as to prevent the Iranian revolution's ideology from spreading to Iraqi Shia. Instead of a quick victory, this became a brutal eight-year war of attrition that devastated both countries, resulting in an estimated half a million casualties among soldiers and a similar number among civilians. The final cost surpassed half a trillion dollars, leaving Iraq insolvent. Kuwait had repeatedly provided loans during the war but was not prepared to forgive the debt, refusing Organization of the Petroleum Exporting Countries (OPEC) oil production cuts intended to raise the oil price for Iraq, which was losing billions of dollars per year due to low prices.

As tensions escalated, Saddam accused Kuwait of economic warfare and drilling diagonally across the border to steal Iraqi oil reserves. Then, on 2 August 1990, after months of sabre-rattling, he launched an invasion. Most of Kuwait was occupied within a day, and hundreds of thousands of Kuwaitis fled abroad. The invasion was widely condemned; even some of Iraq's traditional allies turned against it.

After several ignored UN resolutions and failed peace negotiations, the US launched a military intervention to liberate Kuwait in January 1991. The defeated Iraqi army retreated, setting fire to over 600 Kuwaiti oil wells in revenge during the process. The wells burned for months, causing massive environmental damage and over $20 billion in losses. During the retreat, Iraq also fired dozens of Scud missiles at Israel—a desperate attempt to change the narrative of an out-of-control despot being pacified to one of Palestinian liberation, in the hope of drawing in other Arab nations to defend them.

For the first decade of his rule, Saddam's relations with Western nations had in fact been cordial, and weapons flowed freely from the US during the war with Iran. But in his 2002 'apology' letter to the Kuwaiti people, he wove a pitiable tale of foreigners conspiring against their Arab nation. He told them that he wished for Kuwait only what he wished for himself— 'that foreigners not control you, your wealth or your destiny'— stating that Kuwait was still under direct occupation by American soldiers, who would 'desecrate your soul, minds and religion, except for those who bear arms and resist'.[16]

THE VICIOUS TRIANGLE

Cowards with Weapons

Saddam's impulsive declaration of war against a former ally was standard dictator behaviour, but his refusal to pull back when even his own generals warned him that they couldn't defend Kuwait was unusually reckless. Military strength had always been glorified in Saddam's family; he had grown up on tales of heroic relatives who gave their lives fighting foreign invaders. Decades later, this machismo was still on show. 'I know I am going to lose, but at least I will have the death of a hero,' he told visiting envoys, choosing military defeat over political defeat. Saddam had poured Iraq's wealth and scientific expertise into military technology and once maintained the fourth-largest standing army in the world. After the First Gulf War, the UN passed Resolution 687, calling for the destruction or removal of Iraq's chemical, biological, and nuclear weapons, which Saddam had been developing in extensive programmes since the early 1980s. A commission was created to inspect weapons facilities, setting off a long saga of Iraqi government interference in and obstruction of the investigation and disarmament process.

During the twelve-year interlude between the two Gulf Wars, Iraq was diminished from a regional power centre to an isolated pariah state with a stunted economy. The population suffered under crippling international sanctions and a no-fly zone, unable to import even medicines and basic equipment. Despite this, Saddam's anti-imperialist rhetoric remained belligerent. He declared repeatedly his intention to start a new war to liberate the Palestinian people and destroy Israel, and spoke proudly about sovereignty, despite his once-eminent nation being left with none. He rejected several opportunities to step down peacefully—including two golden parachutes from the UAE's Sheikh Zayed—and clung to power.

Finally, in 2003, the US invasion of Iraq brought Saddam's rule to an end. For twenty-four years, the presidency of one of the region's most anti-imperialist rulers had bought Iraq an almost-constant state of war, ending with the complete and direct US occupation of the country. Hundreds of thousands died, and the country's economy, infrastructure, and education system were left in ruins. In his time as president, the only unequivocally successful military campaign Saddam had conducted was against his own people, when he crushed popular uprisings in 1991, killing tens of thousands. After the end of Iraq's direct occupation by the US in 2011, the country came under the political control of Iran, the very foe Saddam had entered into war to push back in the first place.

Saddam remains an icon to some people in the Arab world, but he should be remembered as the anti-imperialist hero who was God's gift to imperialists. He initiated one of the most pointless and self-defeating wars of the twentieth century in 1980, crippling two countries. He massacred his own people, maintained weapons that were a threat to the world, and engaged in rhetoric and behaviour that made him seem unstable and unhinged—his tyranny eventually standing as a justification for American invasion and occupation.

The Project for American Hegemony

On the American side, the idea of invading Iraq was not new. During the 1991 Gulf War, hard-liners in the Bush administration had urged the American president to pursue the Iraqi army all the way to Baghdad and depose Saddam. Several members of Bush Senior's staff considered this 'unfinished business' after he left office, and continued to organise politically. In 1997 they formed a think tank called Project for a New American Century (PNAC) to systemise advocacy for their foreign policy agenda. They pushed for more US presence in the Middle East and large increases in military spending to ensure the capability of the US to 'rapidly deploy and win multiple large-scale simultaneous wars'. In 1998, President Bill Clinton signed into law the Iraq Liberation Act, which members of PNAC had played a key role in drafting for Congress. It made it official US policy to 'support efforts to remove the regime headed by Saddam Hussein from power in Iraq.'

Of PNAC's twenty-five founding members, ten went on to serve in the cabinet of George W. Bush in 2001, including Vice President Dick Cheney, Secretary of Defense Donald Rumsfeld, and Deputy Secretary of Defense Paul Wolfowitz. Rumsfeld raised the possibility of going after Iraq just two hours after the 9/11 attacks, asking whether this presented an 'opportunity' to attack Iraq the next day. On 20 September 2001, PNAC sent a letter to the US president advocating 'a determined effort to remove Saddam Hussein from power in Iraq'.

Senior officials, including the heads of the CIA and the Defense Intelligence Agency, had said that Saddam's military ambitions had been effectively constrained by the UN sanctions. Saddam 'has not developed any significant capability with respect to weapons of mass destruction,' Secretary of State Colin Powell said in early 2001, emphasising to the Senate three months later that:

> The Iraqi regime militarily remains fairly weak. It doesn't have the capacity it had ten or twelve years ago. It has been contained. And even though we have no doubt in our mind that the Iraqi regime is pursuing programs to develop weapons of mass destruction ... the best intelligence estimates suggest that they have not been terribly successful.

However, Powell continued to build the case for invasion, asserting a year later that 'there's no doubt that Saddam Hussein now has weapons of mass destruction.' In the UK, MI6 claimed in 2002 that Iraq was able to deploy weapons of mass destruction within forty-five minutes of an order. Saddam was linked to the

9/11 attackers and to an attempt to purchase 500 tonnes of concentrated uranium powder for a nuclear weapons programme, based on documents later dismissed as fabrications. He was portrayed as an imminent threat to the West and an active backer of world terrorism directly linked to Al-Qaeda. Claims with no intelligence backing, or contrary to intelligence findings, were repeatedly made at the highest level.

Former US treasury secretary Paul O'Neill later stated that use of force was being considered to oust Saddam from early 2001, with contractors being suggested for post-Saddam oil deals. A British cabinet memo from 2002 indicates that Bush had already made the decision to invade, and 'the intelligence and facts were being fixed around the policy'.[17]

Barack Obama's autobiography *The Audacity of Hope* summarises the rest:

> The PR strategy worked; by the fall of 2002, a majority of Americans were convinced that Saddam Hussein possessed weapons of mass destruction, and at least 66 percent believed (falsely) that the Iraqi leader had been personally involved in the 9/11 attacks. Support for an invasion of Iraq—and Bush's approval rating—hovered around 60 percent. With an eye on the midterm elections, Republicans stepped up the attacks and pushed for a vote authorizing the use of force against Saddam Hussein. And on October 11, 2002, twenty-eight of the Senate's fifty Democrats joined all but one Republican in handing to Bush the power he wanted.[18]

The US went to war.

American hawks had long desired more military presence in the Middle East, and Saddam provided the perfect pretext, all the while imagining himself to be a hero. As his attorney Najib al-Nuaimi put it upon delivering the news that the Iraqi Special Tribunal would sentence him to execution: 'You are the last card to be played by Bush and Blair ... because Bush and Blair have no reasons to invade Iraq. All the claims were against Iraq—you know, nuclear, link with Al-Qaeda—all these stuff has actually disappeared [*sic*] ... But they have you, and you are the one who they will claim, "We have removed the dictator."'[19]

The Iran Nuclear Deal

'We shall export our revolution to the whole world,' declared Ayatollah Khomeini after taking power in Iran in 1979. The Islamic revolution had deposed the Shah, a repressive and despised dictator who became an absolute ruler thanks to a US-organised coup over twenty-five years earlier. When the US allowed the Shah to seek safety in New York after the revolution, furious mobs stormed the US embassy in Tehran, starting a year-long hostage crisis.

Over the next decades, hostility between the US and the Islamic Republic of Iran continued to rage. The US accused Iran of sponsoring terrorism across the world in the 1990s and imposed an embargo in 1995, making Iran a pariah state. In his State of the Union address in 2002, President George W. Bush famously listed Iran as part of an 'axis of evil', along with Iraq and North Korea. In August that year, defectors revealed Iran's secret programme to develop nuclear weapons. Iran agreed to halt uranium enrichment in 2004, but a year later, populist Mahmoud Ahmadinejad was elected president and restarted the programme.

Despite tensions, war was not on the menu. The Iraq War— the most intractable conflict for America since Vietnam—had cost the US over $2 trillion and 35,000 wounded or killed soldiers, leaving the US public in no mood for another war. On an anti-war platform, Barack Obama was elected president in 2008 and promised that he would bring the troops home.

The War Lobby

Israeli Prime Minister Benjamin Netanyahu didn't recognise this attitude shift in the American leadership and among the public—or if he did, he didn't let it stop him. He continued calling on the US to strike Iran, insisting that 'the price of an attack is far lower than the price of inaction', and that there was no option remaining but military force. In 2009, Netanyahu told a visiting US Congress delegation that Iran was 'probably one or two years away' from nuclear weapons capability and, later that same year, that it could already make 'one bomb'. These warnings became a fixture of his annual speeches at the UN; in 2012 he theatrically brandished a cartoon bomb diagram with a lit fuse to explain that Iran would be able to construct a weapon within one year. Another speech earlier that year made the timeline only 'a few months'.[20]

But there was another reason Netanyahu wasn't being taken seriously; he and other Israeli leaders had been making the same warnings for over two decades. In 1992, he told the Israeli Knesset that Iran was 'three to five years' away from nuclear weapons capability, and that this threat had to be 'uprooted by an international front headed by the US.' He repeated this claim in his 1995 book *Fighting Terrorism*, and in 1996 appeared before the US Congress to convey his warnings. Throughout the whole period, official positions of leading figures in the US and Israeli military establishments, as well as the International Atomic Energy Agency, held that Iran was not developing nuclear weapons. Even Netanyahu's own intelligence officials seemed to repeatedly belie his claims.

Netanyahu's credibility was also not helped by the fact that he had been a vocal proponent of the Iraq invasion. In 2002, he had testified under oath before a US Congress committee that, 'There is no question whatsoever that Saddam is seeking and is working and is advancing towards the development of nuclear weapons'—a claim disproven after the invasion.[21]

In 1998, Donald Rumsfeld had also told Congress that Iran would have the bomb by 2003—neoconservatives in the Bush administration who had argued for war in Iraq were hawkish on Iran too, and it was considered to be part of the same project. But a decade later, others were starting to fear the possibility of war. The chairman of the US Joint Chiefs of Staff, General Martin Dempsey, publicly stated in 2012 that he did not want to be complicit if Israel chose to carry out a strike on Iran. The retired Israeli chief of staff and the director of Mossad were claiming that, two years earlier, Netanyahu had attempted to order the country to 'full attack readiness', and only their refusal had prevented it. 'Mr Netanyahu is obsessed with an Israeli attack on Iran,' said former defence minister Shaul Mofaz. 'In the seventy days that I sat in government, more than half the meetings that Mr Netanyahu arranged with me were spent in attempts to persuade me we should attack Iran without American or Western support.'[22]

In America, pressure continued to mount—Republican presidential primary candidates universally took a tough stance on Iran, with candidate Mitt Romney stating his complete acceptance of the Israeli assessment of the threat. As titles such as 'Time to Attack Iran' appeared in the *National Review* and other publications, polling data showed that over half of Americans now supported stopping Iran's nuclear programme even if it meant military action. As Obama entered his second term in office, he felt pressured to take the option of war off the table before it was too late.

A Deal in an Echo Chamber

Five rounds of escalating UN sanctions between 2008 and 2012—plus more from the UK, the US, and Canada in 2011—crippled the Iranian economy. The country's oil industry had previously provided as much as 80 per cent of public revenues; bans on purchasing Iranian oil were a severe blow, costing $160 billion in lost revenue over four years. Between 2011 and 2013 alone, Iran's currency lost two thirds of its value. Due to a combination of both economic pressure on the government and political pressure from the population, whose cost of living rose drastically, the regime came to the negotiating table to discuss abandoning its nuclear weapons programme. In 2013, Hassan Rouhani, perceived to be more inclined to negotiations and less aggressively anti-Western than Ahmadinejad, won decisively in presidential elections.

Proponents of the Iran nuclear deal used this opportunity, as well as the extreme position of Netanyahu, to set up a false choice—between a deal, at any cost, and war. 'Obama and Iran's Rouhani Must Seize the Moment In Spite of Hardliners,' wrote a member of the National Iranian American Council, an organisation which had for years lobbied for the lifting of sanctions on Iran.[23] The NIAC kept quiet about human rights abuses in Iran, instead working together with the Obama administration to create a media climate highly favourable to the nuclear deal. 'We created an echo chamber,' said Ben Rhodes, Obama's deputy national security adviser for strategic communications; seemingly independent experts 'were saying things that validated what we had given them to say.'[24] In Rhodes's narrative, amplified by the echo chamber of friendly journalists, there were two sides of the Iranian regime—hard-liners and moderates—and the newly elected 'moderate' President Rouhani was offering a historic window of goodwill in which to negotiate peace. In this binary echo chamber, those who didn't agree with the premise or scope of the negotiations, or who raised concerns about human rights, were simply smeared as warmongers. The middle position was treated as if it didn't exist. Native human rights activists may not always be right, but their voices should be heard and considered, not shut down and ignored as if they don't matter.

On the receiving end of this gaslighting campaign were Iranian civil society activists who had worked for decades to promote human rights in their country. Maryam Nayeb Yazdi, a Canadian-Iranian campaigner for political prisoners, described how activists were targeted by sustained campaigns to discredit their work and prevent their criticism from affecting the Iran deal. 'They spread the idea that talking about human rights would anger the regime and make them more extreme. Somehow the best way to support human rights was by not mentioning them—which of course was nonsense.'[25] Nayeb Yazdi was running a campaign to get Saeed Malekpour, a political prisoner, off death row. 'People were saying ridiculous things like, you're trying to get the US to go to war with Iran for one person—that's how paranoid they were!' Media interest in Nayeb Yazdi's case dried up overnight. Other activists also reported being frozen out. 'The [Obama] administration basically kept us at arm's length. They didn't invite us to express our opinion or share our expertise anymore, they stopped inviting us to their annual Norooz [Persian New Year] events,' said another Iranian activist. Another institute, the Boroumand Center, started a database in 2006 to document human rights violations in Iran, resulting in a record of over 20,000 cases. Its co-founder Roya Boroumand remarked, 'The rhetoric of regime apologists was, "You want Iran to be bombed!"'[26]

In 2009, hundreds of thousands of Iranians took to the streets to protest against fraudulent elections, in what became known as the Persian Spring, or Green Revolution. When they were met with heavy repression, the US response was surprisingly muted. 'Obama, Obama, are you with them or with us?' Iranians chanted, in reference to his disillusioning silence on human rights. According to administration officials, 'We were still trying to engage the Iranian government and we did not want to do anything that made us side with the protesters.'[27] In Boroumand's view, 'The biggest harm Western governments can do is stay silent. If Iran is at the negotiation table, it's because they need it. So you can talk about the fact that people are being prosecuted without lawyers—these are facts.' She continued, 'Every activist will tell you that visibility means safety. Disappearing means that you are at the mercy of the abusers.'

In 2015 the negotiations succeeded, and the deal was signed—the Joint Comprehensive Plan of Action (JCPOA). It stipulated that Iran would decrease the size of its uranium stockpile by 98 per cent and limit enrichment levels for fifteen years, as well as allowing inspections. But the deal came at a grave cost for Iranians and residents of the entire region. Empowered by the international community turning a blind eye to human rights abuses, Iran ramped up its execution rate to over 1,000 in 2015—a fourfold increase on the previous year—and increased its support for Syria's Assad regime, committing brutal war crimes.

The Iran deal prevented war between the US and Iran, but fuelled the Iranian regime's wars across the region—a catastrophic outcome for those calling for regional peace. Ironically it was the warmongering rhetoric and militarism that created the situation of alarmism in which it was possible to pass such a bad deal; in their urgency to take down the Iranian regime, Netanyahu and other hawks strengthened their enemy's hand. Their extremism and zeal for war made the Ayatollahs appear as the responsible and moderate party, pushing the world's powers towards them.

However, this interplay is not limited to the negotiation of the Iran deal in 2013–2015. The sanctions that the country was placed under were also a form of foreign intervention, and arguably strengthened the regime by hurting its population badly. They had impaired the middle class, who are essential to the development of civil society, and the greatest internal challenge for authoritarian regimes. They also allowed the regime to present itself internally as defending the country from external aggression. We'll discuss the efficacy of sanctions as a means to pressure authoritarian regimes in later chapters.

When Donald Trump became US president in 2016, he upped the anti-Iran rhetoric. His administration repeatedly condemned the JCPOA and announced America's withdrawal from the deal in May 2018. This again allowed Iran to position itself as the reasonable party and left European diplomats scrambling to save the deal, rather than to pressure Iran on human rights. Meanwhile, Netanyahu continues to urge harsh action on Iran at every opportunity—'a cartoonish circus which does not even deserve a response,' according to Iranian Foreign Minister Mohammad Javad Zarif. Speaking in support of the nuclear deal at the Munich Security Conference in February 2018, Russian Senator Aleksey Pushkov said that scrapping the agreement was akin to choosing between war and peace, showing that the same binary continued to hold sway: either unconditionally legitimise an authoritarian regime, or declare war.[28]

* * *

Consent is the currency of state-building, and no regime can continue for any amount of time without the acquiescence of the population—not even dictatorships. But tyrants obtain consent differently—instead of through the choice of the population, they extract it through intimidation, bribery, tribalism, and violence. Fights against a perceived foreign enemy are a great opportunity for regimes to re-entrench themselves, seeking domestic support and foreign sympathy. In response to external threats, both Saddam and the Iranian regime promoted themselves to their people as the only counterweight to foreign attack. Yet, despite their fearmongering and nationalistic posturing, belligerent tyrants also provide a perfect opportunity for foreign intervention—so often has 'spreading democracy' been an excuse to invade and control a country that it has become a trope.

Instead of damaging a regime, foreign intervention can make it more secure and reduce internal pressure against it. Research has shown that we're more tolerant of authoritarianism when we're scared.[29] Dissent decreases, and consent is more easily extracted by those in power. The threat of war in 2012 pushed Iranian civil society to divert some of its efforts towards trying to prevent it, instead of focusing on human rights abuses. Moreover, sanctions made the Iranian people have to pay more for essential items, lowered the standard of living, and removed the comfort and resources that allow people to engage in and fund activism.

Terrorists and Foreign Intervention

In the final dynamic of the triangle, we'll examine the nexus between terrorists and foreign military interventions. Whilst this may seem perverse to many citizens of Western countries, it is an instinctive comparison to those who have suffered under both. Both are characterised by the use of violence to seize power or attain policy outcomes; often foreign intervention uses the same methods as terrorist groups with more sophistication and less secrecy, carried out by larger and better-equipped forces.

We will look at two examples. In the first, US intervention in Iraq feeds terrorism through a combination of ignorance, incompetence, and arrogant complacency. In the second, we see how Palestinian militancy served to justify Israel's subjugation of the Palestinians.

The Iraq War: A Hotbed of Terror

Terrorism and tyranny were the two justifications for one of the most costly and destructive wars of the twenty-first century, the US invasion of Iraq. As we have seen, claims that Iraq was harbouring terrorists formed part of the justification—as quickly as three days after the 9/11 attacks, Bush administration figures were trying to find a way to link Iraq to Al-Qaeda, despite intelligence failing to support this claim. Nine days after the attacks, President Bush declared a war on terror, and less than two years later, Iraq became 'the central front in the war on terror'.[30]

The 2003 invasion began with a 'shock and awe' campaign involving a multi-pronged ground assault and a relentless air campaign. It succeeded in toppling Saddam's regime in less than three weeks, and as the Iraqi army crumbled and the regime's central leadership went into hiding, an end to major operations was declared. Then, as the state collapsed into anarchy, the insurgency began. Initially, small guerrilla units—many including former members of the Iraqi military—carried out small attacks with assault rifles, RPGs and roadside improvised explosive devices. They grew in frequency, audacity, and quality of planning and execution, with the units attempting to ambush US troops and firing mortars at bases.

Foreign domination has been one of the most powerful motivations to fight throughout human history, and Iraq was no different. The insurgency rapidly expanded from a fightback by regime elements to a fierce anti-occupation cause. It found parallels in recent Iraqi history, with the country's nationalisation of its oil industry and expulsion of British colonial interests still within living memory, and was exacerbated by religious populists, who pushed the angle of non-Muslim troops invading a Muslim country to destroy Islam.

The insurgency was exacerbated by the blunders and authoritarian rule of the transitional government, the Coalition Provisional Authority (CPA). When he was parachuted in as the CPA's administrator, Paul Bremer knew no Arabic and had no experience of Iraq or the Middle East. After early remarks about the need to privatise industry (in the middle of a warzone), Bremer issued the first two CPA orders: the banning of the Ba'ath Party in all its forms, and the dissolution of the Iraqi military, security, and intelligence infrastructure. The first order began the de-Ba'athification process, removing anyone who had ever worked for the old regime in any capacity from their positions and banning them from public sector jobs in future, effectively making them unemployable. The second order caused over half a million men, who had military training and experience but few other skills, to become unemployed overnight. These two orders were an unmitigated catastrophe, leading hundreds of thousands of dismissed Iraqi soldiers, humiliated and angry, into the insurgency.

As time wore on and Saddam's weapons of mass destruction were not found, America's justifications for the war shifted. Fighting terrorism became the war's primary cause—the occupation was being extended in order to wipe out the insurgency against the occupation. While experts warned that the continued American presence was radicalising fighters and turning Iraq into a magnet for foreign jihadists, Bremer initially insisted that insurgents were only Saddam loyalists—contradicting his country's administration, who had been selling the invasion as a chance to disrupt regional terror networks.[31] As the occupation continued, the insurgency worsened. 'Stuff happens ... freedom is untidy,' said Secretary of Defense Donald Rumsfeld in response to reports that entire ministries had been decimated by looting.[32] What was to come wouldn't be Bremer's problem—he retired after fourteen months at the CPA's helm, later saying, 'It felt good to get out. ... I said to the new Iraq leaders: "You have your republic—now make it work."'[33]

Grievance

Iraqis watched helplessly as incompetent, arrogant, and corrupt foreigners dismantled their country and destroyed its infrastructure. Bremer had shunned UN assistance, insisting that their experience in stabilisation and reconstruction was unnecessary, even as the occupation failed to provide basic services such as clean water, sanitation, and electricity. In 2005, auditors revealed that around $9 billion allocated for reconstruction had disappeared.[34]

But it was the violence that created real shockwaves of rage across Iraq, the region, and the entire Muslim world. Among the abuses US troops committed were violence against prisoners and civilians, torture, reprisal killings, and unrestrained use of force. There are so many incidents from the eight-year occupation that it would be impossible to list them all, but a sample is necessary.

In April 2003, a month after the occupation began, US soldiers fired into a crowd of Iraqi civilian protesters in Fallujah, killing seventeen and wounding at least seventy. A similar incident had taken place two weeks earlier in Mosul, leading to ten Iraqi civilian deaths and scores of injuries. In both cases, US soldiers claimed they had been returning hostile fire, though a Human Rights Watch investigation in the first case and Iraqi witnesses in the second brought no evidence of this. When US forces bombed a wedding in the village of Mukaradeeb in 2004, military leadership denied any wrongdoing—the deputy chief of staff insisted that 'we operated within our rules of engagement', and Major General James Mattis pointed out the presence of 'military-age males' as justification that the gathering was a legitimate target. Forty-five civilians were killed, including women and children.

In November 2005, a roadside bomb targeted a US Marine convoy near Haditha Dam, killing one Marine and injuring two others. In response, the Marines went on a rampage. They ordered the occupants of a passing taxi to get out and executed them in the street, before methodically searching nearby houses and killing twenty-four civilian occupants, including a seventy-six-year-old man in a wheelchair and six terrified children huddled together. To cover up their massacre, they reported that fifteen had died in a bomb blast and the remainder were insurgents killed in a subsequent firefight.

In March 2006, four American soldiers entered the Janabi family home in Al-Mahmudiya in the middle of the day and killed the parents and younger sister of fourteen-year-old Abeer al-Janabi, before gang-raping her, then shooting her in the head and burning her body. The soldiers blamed the massacre on Sunni insurgents, but three months later a fellow soldier brought their war crimes to light.

In the Hamdania incident, US Marines abducted a man during a raid and placed him in a hole in the road, his hands and feet bound. They then retreated a short distance and opened fire on him, while other members of the group shot a stolen Iraqi AK-47 in the air to make it sound as though a gunfight were taking place. The group of Marines then unbound the man's corpse, scattered the expended AK-47 bullets around the area, and left a shovel beside the body to frame the man as a militant planting a roadside bomb.

Many of these incidents were dismissed as isolated events, but they were regular and interspersed with a constant flow of daily abuses. Veterans describe jumpy or trigger-happy soldiers opening fire on cars as they turned corners towards surprise checkpoints. Supply convoys to US military bases travelled with wanton disregard for Iraqi lives, speeding through densely populated residential areas, ignoring traffic signals, and frequently running over and killing civilians. Former soldiers describe firing shots at any civilian cars in their way, sometimes merely for 'driving too close'. Incidents of death were so numerous that many were never reported.

'You physically could not do an investigation every time a civilian was wounded or killed because it just happens a lot and you'd spend all your time doing that,' said one Marine. 'I guess while I was there, the general attitude was, a dead Iraqi is just another dead Iraqi,' another soldier said.[35] The Iraq War Documents leak in 2010 revealed approximately 15,000 civilian deaths that had not previously been admitted by the US government, and a failure to investigate hundreds of reports of abuse, torture, rape, and murder.[36]

In April 2004, over a thousand photographs came to light that revealed US soldiers' systematic physical and sexual abuse of Iraqi prisoners in Abu Ghraib prison. The mildest showed techniques of 'enhanced interrogation' (torture), which were in widespread use in American detention centres inside and outside Iraq and had been approved at the highest levels of US government. Other photographs revealed extreme, sadistic abuse—including rape of men, women, and children—which had been perpetrated against thousands of prisoners, vast numbers of whom were in prison for no reason by the guards' own admission. Naked, emaciated detainees were hooded and piled into human pyramids, electrocuted with car batteries, held on leashes like dogs, forced to strip and crawl around, and ridden by soldiers like animals. Soldiers posed, grinning, in many of the grotesque images, even holding thumbs up beside corpses.

The Abu Ghraib images caused a storm around the world, opening discussions of abuse of power and war crimes. Their impact across the Arab world and on the Muslim psyche globally was even more concentrated. We recall vividly the plight of Muslims in Iraq being a fixture of every Friday sermon in our teens and twenties, fury and helplessness vocalised in fiery supplications for the destruction of tyrannical occupiers. The narrative of extremist recruiters was the same—that America and the West were fighting a new crusade, a dirty war against Islam itself, in which there were no rules or rights.

Fitting the Jihadist Narrative

In the early 2000s, taking stock of the successes and failures of his wider cause in past decades, jihadist strategist Abu Musab al-Suri wrote a 1,600-page master text titled *The Global Islamic Resistance Call*. He noted how difficult it was to convince the Muslim masses to take up arms against their nominally Muslim rulers, or to start a civil war against their Muslim compatriots. But at the same time, the Soviet invasion of Afghanistan and ongoing occupation of Palestine saw Muslims display immense bravery and willingness to take up arms against foreign intervention. As we saw in Chapter 1, al-Suri saw great value in situations where there were invaders on the ground at home, viewing this as one way to incite a popular jihad.

Al-Qaeda started to goad the US into invading the Muslim world, with actions such as the 1998 bombings of US embassies in East Africa and the 2000 bombing of the USS Cole in Yemen. After the 9/11 attacks, they knew that they had succeeded, and began moving their families to safe places in anticipation of the invasion of Afghanistan. In February 2003, shortly before the invasion of Iraq, Bin Laden issued a message to Iraqis about how to fight the Western crusaders.[37] In October, he told his followers, 'Be glad of the good news: America is mired in the swamps of the Tigris and Euphrates ... here is America today being ruined before the eyes of the whole world.'[38] 'The Americans took the bait and fell into our trap!' another Al-Qaeda commander, Seif al-Adl, gloated.[39] A letter from Al-Qaeda's leadership to its commander in Iraq, Abu Musab al-Zarqawi, stated, 'The most important thing is that the jihad continues with steadfastness ... indeed, prolonging the war is in our interest.'[40]

Warned that Iraq would become a jihadist magnet, the complacent US administration did little. The American occupation of Iraq rescued the jihadist movement just when many of its critics, and even its members, thought it was finished. Far from combatting extremism, the Iraq War brought a decade of insurgency and civil war, and ultimately ISIS.

THE VICIOUS TRIANGLE

Terrorist University

During the invasion, US forces swept up large numbers of military-aged Iraqis from the streets and from their homes during raids—often working on flawed tip-offs or on no basis at all—and sent them to prisons indefinitely. Abu Ghraib shot to world attention in 2004, but an even larger warehouse of prisoners would also later become infamous—Camp Bucca, the birthplace of ISIS.

The 26,000 men held at Camp Bucca included members of the old Saddam regime, as well as ordinary civilians caught in the wrong place at the wrong time, unjustly detained and seething with anger towards their captors. In the prison, these inmates freely mixed with religious fanatics from the insurgency, many of whom were veterans of the battlefields of Afghanistan. 'Extremists had freedom to educate the young detainees,' one former detainee described later. 'I saw them giving courses using classroom boards on how to use explosives, weapons—and how to become suicide bombers.' Radicalisation, recruitment, and training happened right under the American guards' noses.[41]

Seventeen of the twenty-five most important leaders of ISIS spent time in US prisons between 2004 and 2011, including Ibrahim Awad al-Badri—later to become Abu Bakr al-Baghdadi.[42] Another, Haji Bakr, was a former colonel in Saddam's air force who had no prospect of future work after the CPA's first orders. He threw in his lot with fellow prisoners and used his experience to draw up the entire organisational structure of ISIS, as well as the strategies that led to its early success.

Eventually, the prison started to use crude tests to sort inmates by how radicalised they were. Now the worst of the worst were together. 'We could never have all got together like this in Baghdad, or anywhere else,' one jihadist later told journalists. 'It would have been impossibly dangerous. Here, we were not only safe, but we were only a few hundred metres away from the entire Al-Qaeda leadership.' He continued, 'We had so much time to sit and plan. It was the perfect environment.'[43] By 2007, even the new commander of the prison, Marine Major General Doug Stone, realised how important the prison had become for jihadists—they were deliberately allowing themselves to be captured in order to join their comrades. 'They showed up knowing about our intake process,' Stone said. 'They would come in and say, "I believe this and such and therefore I'd like to get into Compound 34." These guys were using detention for their own purposes.'[44]

In 2009, as the occupation drew to an end, the prison was closed. Prisoners who had not been accused were released, and many of those transferred to the Iraqi government subsequently escaped in high-profile prison breaks engineered by the Islamic State of Iraq. They rejoined the insurgency with improved tactics. When the brutal clampdown on the Syrian revolution created large swathes of ungoverned territory in Syria, they hopped the border—under the watchful eye of Assad—and declared an Islamic State. With the equipment they conquered from Syrian bases, they returned and rapidly overran half of Iraq.

* * *

The overall record of the occupation of Iraq is a dire one. The Americans installed a chronically corrupt and dysfunctional government with a severe legitimacy deficit, purging state institutions of all who had served the previous regime in even the most minor capacity. Legions of unemployed and unemployable men were left, many of whom had extensive military experience. They held deep grudges from the brutality of the occupation, which had effectively amounted to an all-out war against Iraqi civilians. These grudges were mirrored in the wider population, along with severe trauma and desensitisation to violence.

The stream of shocking images of American soldiers abusing helpless Muslim men and women in grotesque ways made better recruitment material than any extremist could have dreamed, vindicating the jihadist narrative just as Al-Qaeda had predicted. Thousands were radicalised across the world in the 2000s, and Iraq became a beacon for jihadists worldwide, just as the occupation's prisons became their incubators. And then the US left, declaring its mission accomplished. It bequeathed the region to its allies, who continued the same security-focused policies, as well as using the cover of a war on terror to silence political adversaries.

Nouri al-Maliki, Iraq's corrupt and sectarian prime minister, would put down popular protests with military force—the culmination of a series of policies that attempted to disenfranchise and marginalise the Sunni community of Iraq, creating a situation that was conducive to radicalisation. As the 2011 uprisings spread across the MENA, the Obama administration did little to support the democratic aspirations of people in the region or to protect them from tyrants, including those who happened to be US allies. A historic opportunity to end the appeal of terrorism without military force passed by, and clashes grew into a security vacuum, into which ISIS appeared. The Iraqi army collapsed in front of it, and global terrorism reached new heights. After a trillion dollars and fifteen years, the war on terror had taken extremism from a small flame that could have gone out alone to a blazing conflagration. The triangle continued to turn.

Invasions create insurgencies, and the presence of each justifies the other. American neoconservatives were looking for a reason to invade Iraq, and Bin Laden's Al-Qaeda needed a foreign occupier in order to masquerade as a popular resistance movement. During the occupation, American soldiers' crimes against civilians shocked and enraged the entire Muslim world, as good as putting the bullets into the jihadists' guns for them. As icing on the cake, the Americans had even built the world's best terrorist training camp.

THE MIDDLE EAST CRISIS FACTORY

Palestine: The World's Longest-Running Military Occupation

The Israel–Palestine conflict has been militarised since the beginning. Military occupation and ethnic cleansing in the 1940s were followed by two wars between Israel and multiple Arab states in 1967 and 1973. Subsequent decades have seen continuous low-level military resistance from various Palestinian resistance groups, punctuated by major Israeli offensives. But there was a period in which violence wasn't the standard.

Between the 1967 Arab–Israeli War and 1987, Palestinians grew increasingly hopeless. The young and growing population was confined in isolated plots of land. Construction and agriculture were limited, and the stunted economy of the occupied territories couldn't provide jobs or prosperity. Israeli settlements expanded to annex more and more Palestinian territory. The Israel Defense Forces (IDF) regularly carried out detentions without trial, beatings, house demolitions, and retributive extrajudicial killings. For Palestinians, discrimination, intimidation, and humiliation were an everyday reality. Then, in 1987—after a generation of repression—something broke, and the first intifada began.

The First Intifada

Throughout 1987, several large protests had occurred over the shooting, beating, and arrest of students. The spark for the intifada came when several Palestinian labourers were killed by a tank at a checkpoint in December. The funeral turned into a mass protest, and within days, protests had spread across the Palestinian territories. Shopkeepers and labourers went on strike, roads were barricaded with burning tires, and rocks were hurled at Israeli soldiers and military vehicles.

The Israeli response was harsh; tear gas, water cannons, and rubber bullets were used, and riot police attacked protesters with truncheons. Live ammunition was also deployed, and large-scale collective punishment practised, including mass arrests, curfews, the cutting of electricity and water, property confiscations, and home demolitions. When lawyers went on strike in Gaza, the leaders of their union were arrested and held for six months without trial. Palestinian universities and schools were shut down, which meant that children and young people had nothing to do but join in with the protests and riots.

Grassroots Palestinian groups started to coordinate the action early. They came together to form the Unified National Leadership of the Uprising, issuing statements, printing leaflets, and helping to coordinate protests and ensure they were non-violent. They also called for additional forms of protest against the occupation, such as withholding taxes to Israel, and adopted the slogan 'no taxation without representation'.

Early on, lethal tactics were specifically avoided, but an increasing number of violent incidents was committed by groups outside of the Unified National Leadership. In the first year, not a single Israeli died, whilst Israeli soldiers killed 142 Palestinians in Gaza alone.[45] Over the course of the intifada, at least 1,200 Palestinians were killed and tens of thousands injured. This included close to 30,000 children who required medical attention due to injuries they received from beatings within the intifada's first two years, almost a third of them aged ten or under.[46] The ratio of Palestinian to Israeli deaths was slightly more than 3 to 1.

The asymmetry in violence shaped international media coverage; children throwing rocks at tanks became the defining image of the intifada across the world. Israel was the subject of several attempted resolutions by the UN Security Council, all vetoed by the US, and refused to receive UN delegations to investigate. Even staunch allies of Israel struggled to explain its actions—as British MP Gerald Kaufman said, 'Friends of Israel as well as foes have been shocked and saddened by that country's response to the disturbances.'[47]

The pressure of the intifada, together with other global events, forced Israel into peace talks. The Palestine Liberation Organization (PLO) was also ready to negotiate, and leaders of the non-violent resistance became elected members in the group. In 1993, the Oslo Accords were negotiated, and the PLO formally recognised Israel. A two-state solution seemed near.

Disillusionment and Polarisation

After the Oslo Accords were signed, Israel began to withdraw from some areas of the Gaza Strip and the West Bank, and the Palestinian Authority was established to govern them. However, the agreement quickly became deeply unpopular.

The Accords were a partial agreement intended to lead towards further negotiations and a wider peace deal. The timeline they created towards Palestinian statehood relied on three key issues being resolved: settlements, Jerusalem, and the right of return of Palestinian refugees. However, for decades the PLO had led the Palestinian people under the premise that it was fighting to liberate their land, including the coastal area that contained all the major cities that were at the heart of Palestinian identity, which was now being conceded to Israel. On the other side, right-wing Israelis held that Judea and Samaria (the West Bank) is God-given land instrinsically connected to Jewish identity; now, they were being told that they had to give it up. These concessions polarised both sides, and eventually, negotiations and the peace process broke down. Statehood never materialised, and Palestinians became deeply disillusioned.

One of the conditions placed by Israel on the negotiations was that the intifada must stop, and that the PLO must end all coordination for civil disobedience. When it did so, not only did the PLO lose the leverage that had opened the negotiations, but it left the banner of resisting the occupation to other actors who did not believe in non-violence. Hamas, founded during the intifada in 1988, had carried out its first attack the following year and created its military wing, the Qassam Brigades, in the final months of the intifada. In 1993, as non-state violence increased on both sides, Hamas began a campaign of suicide bombings in the West Bank. When an Israeli-American opened fire on men praying in a mosque in Hebron the following year, killing twenty-nine and wounding 125, the Qassam Brigades began to perform suicide attacks inside Israel.

Meanwhile, the Israeli right wing grew and became radicalised. They campaigned against the Oslo Accords and any concession of God-given 'Jewish' land to Palestinians. In 1995, Prime Minister Yitzhak Rabin was assassinated by Yigal Amir, a young ultranationalist extremist. Yigal explained his motivation in a court hearing: 'According to Jewish law, the minute a Jew gives over his people and his land to the enemy, he must be killed. My whole life has been studying the Talmud and I have learnt this.'[48]

The killing symbolised not only a rejection of peace, but also the rise of a new Israeli far right. In the weeks leading up to Rabin's murder, two major rallies had taken place in which protesters branded the prime minister a traitor and called for his death, carrying pictures depicting him as a Nazi and even conducting a mock funeral procession. Benjamin Netanyahu, the leader of the right-wing Likud party, had been a speaker at these rallies.[49] 'Bibi [Netanyahu] is not guilty of Rabin's murder, but he was the main inciter then at [the demonstrations in] Zion Square and in Raanana,' said former prime minister Ehud Barak in 2016.[50] In 1996, a year after Rabin's assassination, Netanyahu became responsible for the peace negotiations upon being elected Israel's prime minister.

The Second Intifada

With the election to government of an uncompromising right-wing coalition headed by Netanyahu, settlement construction on occupied territory resumed. Both sides became entrenched in maximalist positions and, deeply disillusioned by the stalled peace talks, began to prepare militarily for a total breakdown of the negotiations.

In September 2000, despite warnings that it would be provocative, Israeli opposition leader Ariel Sharon visited the Haram al-Sharif complex in Jerusalem with an escort of more than a thousand armed police officers. The site, also referred to as the Temple Mount, is revered by both Jews and Muslims; it had been at the centre of the most contentious part of the peace negotiations, and its final status was yet undetermined. Sharon took the opportunity to declare that it would remain under Israeli control forever. Angry demonstrations broke out immediately, and quickly turned into riots. Protesters threw rocks—and were met with tear gas and rubber bullets. The next day riots escalated, and police switched to live ammunition, killing several young Palestinians and injuring hundreds. After this, Palestinian protests erupted and spread.

As before, the Israeli approach was violent—over a million bullets were fired in the first few days, and French President Jacques Chirac, who attempted to mediate, protested to Prime Minister Ehud Barak about Israel 'firing from helicopters on people throwing rocks'. The killing of Muhammad al-Durrah, a twelve-year-old boy shot dead whilst sheltering behind his father in an alley, was broadcast on television internationally and fuelled rage within Palestine and the wider Arab world.

Over a hundred Palestinians were killed and 6,000 wounded within the first month of the second intifada. Clashes between demonstrators and Israeli police continued, often devolving into not only rock-throwing but also fire-bombing and live fire. A smaller number of Israeli soldiers and civilians were also killed, and airstrikes began against the West Bank and Gaza. Israeli shootings continued to cause large numbers of Palestinian deaths—later investigations found frequent violations of crowd-dispersal protocol, use of excessive force by the IDF, and killings when the Israeli security services were not in danger. The following spring, Ariel Sharon was elected prime minister, again shifting the Israeli government rightward to a more aggressive stance.

Since 1993, Israel had seen at least two to three bombings per year, but the scale was about to radically change. From 2001, Hamas began carrying out rocket attacks aimed at the illegal Israeli settlements and military checkpoints inside the Gaza Strip, and then at surrounding villages in southern Israel. Their low levels of accuracy meant that they were effectively indiscriminate, often causing civilian casualties. Meanwhile, suicide attacks skyrocketed and went from being a fringe tactic to a central weapon of the 'resistance'.

On 1 June 2001, shortly before midnight, a suicide bomber detonated outside the Dolphinarium discotheque, killing twenty-one people queuing to enter and injuring 120 more. Two months later came the Sbarro restaurant bombing, when a pizza restaurant on a main road in Jerusalem was blown up mid-afternoon, killing fifteen people, among them seven children and a pregnant woman, and wounding over 130. These attacks stand out for the callousness of their targets; the Dolphinarium nightclub was popular with teenage girls, and the Sbarro restaurant was known to be frequented by mothers of young children on their way home from school.

It was a deeply damaging period for solidarity with the Palestinian cause. Even liberal Israelis shifted rightward, as the terror attacks turned public opinion in Israel and around the world. 'It was open season on Palestinian journalists,' says Lisa Goldman, a journalist and founding editor of Tel Aviv-based *+972 Magazine*. 'The international media had little time for reporting on Israeli abuses, or the incredibly cruel retaliations innocent civilians suffered ... it was not a message which readers in Europe were amenable to, because of suicide bombings.'[51] For years afterwards, this period was the world's reference point in the conflict, and the narrative generated often made it hard to elicit compassion for Palestinians from Western onlookers.

The IDF placed the headquarters of PLO leader Yasser Arafat under siege in 2002, blaming him for the violence; in a failure of leadership, his Al-Aqsa Brigades had begun to compete with Hamas by conducting their own attacks. After Arafat's death in late 2004, Mahmoud Abbas took charge of the PLO and negotiated a ceasefire deal which de-escalated the intifada. Over the course of four years, around 3,000 Palestinians had been killed, as well as around 700 Israeli civilians and over 200 security personnel. This death toll was double that of the first intifada in a shorter period of time, and though the intifada was considered over, the killings continued afterwards—around 660 Palestinians and 23 Israelis were killed in 2006.

From Occupation to War on Terror

A year after the beginning of the second intifada, Al-Qaeda perpetrated the 9/11 attacks. The entire world was now transfixed by terrorism. Palestinian militants continued their campaign— the period between January 2001 and January 2005 saw only three full months go by without a suicide bombing, and these attacks now became part of a narrative. Rather than having to defend a decades-long occupation against violent resistance, Israel could cast itself as part of the global fight against Islamic terrorism. 'War on terror' rhetoric became the new justification for continued occupation and deprivation of rights, and it succeeded massively.

As early information emerged on the day of the Twin Towers attack, a handful of Palestinians celebrated—America to them was an enemy who supported their occupier. Video recordings of celebrations played on US news networks, and the American public were soon convinced that the United States and Israel faced a common terrorist threat. Only months after President George W. Bush had publicly supported the creation of a Palestinian state and urged Prime Minister Sharon to show restraint with protesters, he was pressured into redoubling his support of the Israeli government. In November 2001, eighty-nine American senators sent Bush a letter demanding that the US not prevent Israel from retaliating against Palestinian violence, and in May 2002, both houses of Congress overwhelmingly passed resolutions affirming their solidarity with Israel and that the two countries were 'now engaged in a common struggle against terrorism'.[52]

Membership in the global war on terror gave Israel a blank cheque to act in ways that would have previously drawn massive resistance. In 2002, Sharon implemented a plan to build a 708-kilometre barrier separating the West Bank from Israel, annexing large amounts of West Bank territory to Israel and restricting the movement of Palestinians. According to Danny Tirza, commander of the military unit that built the wall, 'We had no choice but to build it in order to protect our lives and our children's lives.'[53] The IDF states that the barrier 'serves one purpose and one purpose only: to prevent terrorists from carrying out deadly attacks on Israeli civilians'.[54] Despite these claims, the wall, which has been found to be a violation of international law by the International Court of Justice, had been planned before the intifada or the increase in suicide bombings took place.[55]

Today, it is almost forgotten that the first intifada was intended by its most ardent campaigners to be non-violent, or that into the 1960s a mainstream Palestinian current called for a single democratic state in which all religions and ethnicities would be equal. Acts of desperate, indiscriminate violence that only deepen our crisis should not be glorified or referred to as "resistance". In 2015–2016, a wave of over 166 knife attacks in Israel, largely against civilian targets, fed into Benjamin Netanyahu's narrative perfectly—he has called them 'a new kind of terrorism' and insisted, without any evidence, that they are 'inspired by radical Islam'. A long-time user of 'war on terror' rhetoric, having convened international conferences on terrorism since 1979 and written three books on the subject, Netanyahu weaponises terrorism to delegitimise the entire Palestinian struggle. The term 'terrorists' is regularly applied as a catch-all term for Palestinian prisoners in Israeli prisons, despite the fact that as much as 40 per cent of the adult male Palestinian population has been in some form of Israeli detention since 1967.[56]

Violations of Palestinian rights are justified in Israel in the name of fighting terrorism, whilst peaceful protests—frequently termed 'illegal demonstrations'—are shut down and the people behind them detained, arrested, or judicially intimidated. Issa Amro, a Palestinian activist from Hebron who documents human rights abuses by both Israeli and Palestinian authorities, has faced severe consequences for using non-violent tactics to confront Israeli soldiers and settlers attempting to take over Palestinian homes. He has been repeatedly arrested, detained, threatened, and harassed by authorities, and has even had bones broken. Despite this, he remains a vocal proponent of non-violence. 'They don't want this type of struggle because if there is a non-violent movement it will weaken the occupation. They say the occupation is there for security, but if the struggle is non-violent, then they can no longer justify the occupation.'[57]

Meanwhile, proponents of violence celebrate as 'heroic' the attacks on civilians, believing that these incidents further

Palestinian liberation, when in fact they are giving Israel further justification for its occupation before the world. Issa Amro understands the strategic value to Israel of pushing Palestinian resistance against occupation towards violence—'They want to keep the Palestinians violent so they can kill them.'[58]

* * *

Tens of thousands of Iraqis were arrested and detained during the US occupation. Describing the raids he had conducted on roughly a thousand Iraqi homes, a US veteran recounted:

> You run in. You go up the stairs. You grab the man of the house. You rip him out of bed in front of his wife. You put him up against the wall. ... You'll open up his closet and you'll throw all the clothes on the floor and basically leave his house looking like a hurricane just hit it.

> And if you find something, then you'll detain him. If not, you'll say, 'Sorry to disturb you. Have a nice evening.' So you've just humiliated this man in front of his entire family and terrorized his entire family and you've destroyed his home. And then you go right next door and you do the same thing in a hundred homes.[59]

The raids normally took place in the dead of night, and they bear a striking resemblance to the Israeli raids on Palestinian homes. 'We scared the living Jesus out of them every time we went through every house,' said one Iraq veteran. Israeli soldiers have also stated that this is the point—inflicting humiliation is part of the assignment, the reason for pointless actions such as making detainees strip and wait for hours in their underwear. 'If we go into their houses all the time, if you arrest people all the time, if they feel terrified all the time, they will never attack us.'[60] A bitter irony, then, that this only makes Israel less secure, just like Iraq during the American occupation. As research has shown, large-scale trauma can in fact perpetuate cycles of violence.[61]

Terrorism provides a motivation for occupation—either as the original cause, or by becoming the reason why 'it's not safe to pull out'. But in this symbiotic relationship, foreign occupation reinforces the logic of terrorism—it provides a valid liberation struggle for terrorists to hide behind, creates grievances and oppression narratives to mobilise the population, and inflicts severe trauma which can lead to more violence. This ends up creating 'forever wars', in which the very tactics used to solve problems are the ones making them intractable.

Breaking the Triangle

Tragically, the behaviour of both the occupying forces we've just discussed resembles that of the Egyptian security forces in Sinai. This isn't surprising; a dictatorship is just another occupation, by an internal minority rather than outsiders. The only time terrorists managed to establish a state—ISIS—resulted in just the same tyranny, with draconian policing and relentless targeting of political dissent. Fundamentally, terrorism, tyranny, and foreign intervention all seek to obliterate the agency of the population and use the same oppressive tactics to achieve this. They claim to oppose each other, but the violence they inflict is often no worse than what they are fighting, and the people lose either way—bombed, shot, jailed, tortured, exiled, and killed.

We have seen the story of the century-old merry-go-round of bloodshed and trauma in the Middle East, and the grip of the vicious triangle at its heart. Foreign intervention came first—colonialism robbed the region of its sovereignty. Liberation movements resisted, but their cry for agency was subverted by the tyrants who succeeded to power in post-colonial states. In opposition appeared new liberation movements, but also terrorist groups. Meanwhile, the colonialists never actually left—their intervention took new forms, thus continuing to deny agency to the native population. After 2001, their arm's-length involvement was concretised again, with full-scale invasions and occupations, which re-energised terrorism on a scale not seen before.

Each player in this ecosystem is self-interested, but their interests intersect with each other. As much as terrorists, tyrants, and foreign warmongers despise each other, they agree on a few core things. They prioritised looting, naked theft of resources, and self-enrichment. They believed their ends legitimised any exercise of force, and prioritised the elimination of dissent. And most importantly, they knew better than the native population. Not a single one of them was willing to abide by free and fair democratic elections.

The choice between tyranny, terrorism, and foreign intervention is a false one; they are part of one continuum, and more of one leads to more of the other two. You can never expunge any one alone, because the others will always provide fertile ground for its regrowth. Empowering any side of the triangle means the empowerment of the entire triangle.

We have only discussed a handful of examples of the vicious triangle in action, which could have equally included Afghanistan's journey through the Soviet and American invasions; the Lebanese Civil War; Gaddafi's 'defiance' of the West at the cost of his own population's welfare; the breakdown and then break-up of Sudan; or the stories of Somalia, Turkey, Algeria, or Yemen, each going through the same tragic cycles of terrorism, tyranny, and foreign intervention.

* * *

The Bush years saw the worst of the war on terror, but they were also some of the best days for many of the region's dictators. They had enjoyed excellent relations with the West as well as a muted domestic political scene, easily painting any internal dissent as sympathy for terrorism. Instead of the region's monarchies becoming more democratic, the region's republics were becoming more like monarchies.

But the Bush years would end with a crushing global recession, which hit the oil-dependent MENA region especially hard. As Obama took office, he came with fresh new ideas about ending America's role as global policeman and disengaging from the Bush administration's conflicts. All of a sudden, the region's dictators found themselves in the worst of both worlds—the heyday of the war on terror was over, and the economy was in terrible shape. Unemployment was high, as was corruption, and the ruling elite had no plan or vision beyond preserving their own hold on power. New social media tools were eating at their control over their national media landscapes. Meanwhile, the baby boom of the 1970s was now a youth bulge they did not know how to contain.

On 6 June 2010, one of these millions of youths was hanging out in a cybercafe in Alexandria, Egypt. Two plainclothes police officers barged into the café and demanded to search everyone there. The young man demanded they give a reason for the search or present a legal order—but they wouldn't have that. They beat him savagely inside the café, then took him to a nearby building. There, in front of several witnesses, officers beat him to death. The man's name was Khaled Saeed, and he was twenty-eight years old. Pictures of his mangled face were soon being shared on Facebook, as the story of his murder and the cover-up that followed inflamed anger, and deepened the feeling of powerlessness and humiliation among millions of youth. Elsewhere, Wael Ghoneim, a young Egyptian tech executive, created a Facebook page in solidarity, called 'We are all Khaled Saeed'. Within two weeks, it had gathered over 200,000 members.

The MENA region was about to explode.

3

BREAKAGE

The 2011 uprisings came from the depths of despair. The regimes appeared impregnable, their leaders immortal. Their watchful eyes looked down upon us from posters in every major street and every government office across the region.

Emboldened by powerful allies, many of them Western democracies, they stamped out dissent, restricted freedom of speech, and criminalised political activism. When cornered, they could always appeal to nationalism, anti-imperialism, and religion. In times of crisis, they could cry 'terrorism' and have the world come to their help.

It seemed they were destined to rule us forever. But the facade of stability would soon come crashing down.

By the early 2000s, young people in the Middle East were increasingly literate, educated, and connected both to each other and to the world. But they were also graduating in large numbers and needed jobs—the stagnant, corruption-infested economies had no place for them. The war on terror and the vicious triangle of oppressive powers put these explosive problems on hold, but no attempts were made at actually rooting them out.

This became even more pronounced after the global economic crisis of 2008. By 2010, the unemployment rate in the Arab world averaged 25 per cent—among the highest in the world. At the same time, Arab societies were very young—more than half of the region's population was under the age of twenty-five in 2010.[1] There were other warning signs of instability, which were neglected—Egypt, for example, had seen sporadic but growing protests for several years, and an increasingly active trade union movement. Yet the regimes still appeared to be in total control, with no serious internal opposition. All the way up to the eve of the Arab Spring, the political order—as stagnant and corrupt as it was—seemed to hold.

When a political system becomes unstable, it rarely ever collapses of its own weight; rather, it becomes ever more vulnerable to disaster. Like a house infested with termites, it might still look impressive and upright from afar, until a crisis hits and the whole thing falls apart.

On 17 December 2010, a young man called Mohamed Bouazizi was selling fruit from a fruit cart on the streets of Sidi Bouzid, a small town in Tunisia. On that fateful day, police officers confiscated his cart, slapped him, spat in his face, and then beat him. Bouazizi had been harassed by the police before, but this time he did not have the money to bribe them. Distraught and humiliated by the incident, he rushed to the governor's office to file a complaint, but an official there looked at his still-bloodied face and turned him away. Crushed, humiliated, and hopeless, Bouazizi stepped outside, poured gasoline on his body, and lit himself on fire.

Bouazizi died of his injuries, but not before all of Tunisia had caught fire, too. This one incident, a microcosm of the relationship between the state and the region's youth, galvanised the largest mass protests in the modern history of the Arab world. A little over a month later, the unthinkable happened:

Tunisia's powerful dictator, Zine El Abidine Ben Ali, resigned and fled the country—the Arab Spring had toppled its first government. Tunisia proved something that nobody thought was possible before: The people were not powerless, and if they banded together for long enough, they could force their dictators out of power.

In a matter of days, the region's prolonged crises of legitimacy seemed to come to a head, as the once-stable order snapped. A mere four days after Ben Ali's departure, thousands of people were on the streets in Egypt. The non-violent uprising centred on Cairo's Tahrir Square. The movement had its own martyr, Khaled Saeed—a young man who had been brutally beaten to death by security officers months earlier. Within weeks, Hosni Mubarak, Egypt's 'fourth pyramid', the powerful president of almost thirty years and the linchpin of regional security, had also stepped down. The sense of empowerment was like nothing the region's people had felt before. Emboldened demonstrators took to the streets across the Arab world—in Libya, Syria, Yemen, Bahrain, and beyond. Out of twenty-two Arab countries, all but two—Qatar and the UAE—saw protests.

A barrier of fear had been broken, and the region would never again be the same.

As the revolutions spread in the first few months of 2011, it seemed for a while that countries in the Arab world might share a unified fate. But very soon, each country took its own political path—a reminder that each regime was unique, and each revolution had its own context. After toppling their dictators, Tunisia and Egypt quickly moved into a transitional period. In Bahrain, a swift militarised response from the Gulf Cooperation Council (GCC) restored regime control. In Libya, the uprising against Gaddafi quickly became a civil war that led to international intervention. Yemen and Syria sustained months of protests, as their dictators swayed between stalling and fighting back, with violence gradually rising.

Lots of books have been written on these events—and many more should be written. Our intention here is not to retell that history, but rather to explain what it meant from our vantage point, as participants then who are still living through its legacy a decade later.

The years between 2011 and 2013 were an exceptional period in our region's history. The world was stunned and inspired by the sight of our people on the streets demanding liberty and justice. Old clichés and stereotypes crashed against inspiring scenes of solidarity and courage, and policy makers looked at the region with new eyes, perhaps now able to see the myriad possibilities open.

Since 2013, it has unfortunately become typical to only talk about this early period in terms of how 'it failed'. (It still puzzles us how eager some Western commentators were to argue for our failure—the first time Iyad was invited to join a panel on the 'failure of the Arab Spring' was in July 2011.) But buried under the drab, uninspired analysis are real and important lessons—about revolutions, democratic transitions, and what we accomplished.

A Euphoric Awakening

Popular revolutions aren't merely about protests. What we experienced in 2011 was a political, social, intellectual, and even spiritual awakening. Our region felt like a desert in bloom after a rare rain, proving that it's not dead and showing what is possible.

This isn't to minimise the Arab Spring's political impact, which was immediate. Our people had awakened to their own power, and our dictators shrank in fear, as the entire world took note. A new politics arose, however briefly, in which the 'voice of the streets' could no longer be ignored.

But to look at the uprisings' political impact in isolation ignores what was happening within us—the revival of a profound sense of our direct and personal agency that extended well beyond the political. As natives of the region we felt validated—not as mere political subjects, ideological recruits, or commercial customers, but as agents with responsibility over our intellectual and moral lives, a rediscovered sense of purpose, and a true feeling of dignity.

The sense of camaraderie between us, as well as the feeling of ownership over our public spaces, was palpable and a beauty to watch. It was as though the Middle East we had always dreamed of but thought impossible was suddenly the only real Middle East. Muslims and Christians protected each other as they prayed. Kurds and Arabs, Sunnis and Shia, women and men chanted together for freedom. Citizens cleaned their own streets—streets that suddenly belonged to them, themselves, not the government.

This new florescence extended to the Arabic-language public sphere, which had been moribund for decades, dominated by the monotone of government-approved messages. The online space quickly and organically became the virtual 'city square', where people of all walks of life could discuss their opinions on public matters. Only a few months earlier, these discussions had not only been impossible but would not have been useful, since we had no say in directing our politics or our future. All of a sudden, topics that had once been abstract and theoretical became urgent realities; we now had to question and negotiate values, ideologies, political systems, and social problems. Soon, these conversations developed into campaigns and projects, as groups of like-minded activists started to band together in the borderless spaces created by Facebook and Twitter.

The Arab Spring wasn't like a switch that was flipped on, then off again. It was a real awakening that produced a new citizen in the MENA. Yes—what followed were painful reversals, defeats, and traumas. Many of our friends have fallen, many are in prison; others suffer from debilitating trauma. Many have not regained a sense of normalcy. The lucky became exiles or refugees. But despite all of this, that awakening was real. That citizen is exhausted and traumatised, but still alive, biding their time.

A revolution that came seemingly from nowhere can yet return from nowhere—a fact that only fuels the paranoia of the surviving order.

A Thirty-Year Project

The paradigm that most Western commentators had fresh in their minds when assessing the Arab Spring was the 1989 collapse of the Soviet Union, when a large number of countries previously ruled by autocracies 'joined the free world', embracing the Western model of democracy and, significantly, capitalism. Journalists, analysts, and politicians watching the cascade of revolutions in 2011 expected a similar outcome in the Middle East: a swift adoption of the Western model. This presumption is problematic. In 1989, the Western model enjoyed preeminence, having ultimately triumphed in a decades-long ideological war against its arch-enemy. For post-Soviet states, their alternative to communist authoritarianism was obvious. But 2011 was not 1989. By the time of the Arab uprisings, the so-called Western model was not running victory laps. Instead it was producing one crisis after another, with even its own citizens rejecting it in anti-austerity protests. How could we be expected to embrace the Western model even as its youth were on the streets complaining about how it had failed them? This isn't to say that we didn't want democratic governance—we did, and we still do—but the details in areas of economics, equality, and the proper role of religion would have to be questioned and renegotiated, something that can't happen in a matter of months.

But there is an even more fundamental difference between the contexts of the Arab Spring and the fall of the USSR. The dictatorships that had ruled over the MENA—home to around half a billion people—formed a formidable, interconnected system, legitimised and supported by a number of powerful and wealthy Western nations. By contrast, the autocracies that oppressed Eastern Europe had been opposed, rather than embraced and assisted, by the West.

While being mindful of differences in context, we can find better historical analogies for radical social and political transitions: the French Revolution; the 1848 Spring of Nations in Europe; even the two World Wars by which Western Europe went from being an order of empires to an order of democracies. Here we see that profound changes in the world order tend to be intergenerational affairs; they play out over decades, they're never linear, and they're always traumatic.

It is no small event, in geopolitics or in history, when 500 million people gain their freedom for the first time. Given the scale and scope of the oppressive forces invested in denying them their agency, upturning such an order is not a project of a few short years. It is, rather, a project of a generation. To us, the Arab Spring is a thirty-year historical transition that began in 2011 as the last phase of a long decolonisation. Did it succeed? Did it fail? These are questions to ask circa 2041.

And so, for all the talk of the 'failure of the Arab Spring', the problem was never our region, but rather the unrealistic expectations and faulty historical frameworks of observers. In fairness, many of us had unrealistic expectations too—a lot of us were young, and we did not anticipate the ferocity with which the old order was going to fight back. The years from 2011 to 2013 were very meaningful, but this was also far too short a period for us to effectively organise, write manifestos, or form political parties of a newer generation. The traumatic setback post 2013 was not inevitable, but the expectation that we could build stable democracies in under two years, after three or four decades of suffocating dictatorship, was very unfair.

What We Accomplished

Considering the immensity of the mission, and despite the painful reversals that we will explore in the next chapters, there were many important and lasting achievements from 2011 to 2013. We believe it is worth highlighting the areas where progress was made.

The first was in self-knowledge. Prior to 2011, people mostly kept to their own community-based circles—dictatorships divide and sow mistrust between different groups, so often taking care of your own is a survival strategy. But when you live within your own social bubble, you lose awareness of the grievances, hopes, and lived realities of so many fellow citizens. This results in a weaker society with low self-knowledge, making it less capable of pressuring its government and centring its own demands.

But in 2011—and in the subsequent uprisings since—everyone poured into the same physical spaces, and all of the bubbles burst at once. People from various communities, sects, faiths, ethnicities, and ideologies met face to face, marching hand in hand. Protesters engaged in creative shows of unity. Public spaces were transformed into inclusive spaces for dissent and creative expression. What followed was pure beauty—a sense of solidarity, a unity of destiny, and a reimagining of a more inclusive national identity. When everyone chanted together, 'The people want the fall of the regime!' we were forced to ask ourselves, who are 'the people'?

The reason self-knowledge is important is that colonised people have it taken away from them, creating a crisis of identity that gives rise to other crises in almost every facet of public life.

Reclaiming self-knowledge is thus a key component of building native agency. It's a long shot to try to chart our path into the future if we don't know who we are, or who we want to be. In an ever-deepening quest for answers to these questions, we felt empowered to cast off the narratives that had long been imposed on us, and to unpack our region's various and complex historical, political, socioeconomic, and cultural layers.

This self-discovery did not end at national identity but extended to regional identity as well. Although Arab and Muslim identities both continued to be relevant, the uprisings of 2011 happened after the causes of Arab Nationalism and Islamism were already past their peak. The heyday of Arab Nationalism was in the 1960s, when it was the dominant paradigm governing the region's politics. Islamism, meanwhile, had had a bad decade after 2001, and despite holding power in Sudan, Iran, and Gaza, Islamists no longer had the automatic sympathy of religious Muslims, many of whom had grown to distrust them.

So, what was our overarching identity in 2011? Here we were, across the whole Arabic-speaking world, raising our voices with the same chant: 'The people want the fall of the regime!' We had the impression of having a shared purpose, a sense of unity that had nothing of the chauvinism of Arab Nationalism or the extremism of Islamism. 'The people' did not mean only Libyans or Egyptians or Tunisians, nor only Arabs or Kurds or Amazigh, nor only Muslims or only Christians—but everyone.

Acts of solidarity were common, with Syrian activists chanting in solidarity with Libya, and Yemenis standing in solidarity with Egypt. Notably, this did not clash with or contradict national identities. A Syrian protester felt all the more Syrian when she identified with Libyan protesters, Yemeni activists only more Yemeni as they recorded songs in solidarity with Egypt. There was a profound understanding that every country was its own entity and every revolution its own venture, but that did not take away from the sense of togetherness and joint destiny.

Our unity was not just about solidarity—it was also about strategy. The 2011 moment demonstrated to many of us that the MENA region's dictatorships function as one structure, an integrated ecosystem. It is very difficult to achieve stable democracy in even one country when surrounded by paranoid dictatorships fighting for self-preservation. Our dictators collaborated against us; it only made sense for us to collaborate against them.

Along with learning more about ourselves and each other came the discovery of who the enemy was. Our various dictators had spent decades telling us that they were on our side, defending us against 'them'—the West, the Islamists, the non-Muslims, each other. But in 2011 all of this had crashed. Our aim was squarely on our first and immediate enemies: the dictators.

Equally important was a deeper understanding of the nature of the struggle—that violence was not how we would win, but how we might lose. It's true that the regimes unleashed immense violence on our peaceful uprisings. In Libya, the uprising started with a series of non-violent protests, but quickly descended into a civil war. In Syria, defectors from Assad's army dedicated themselves to protecting protesters, but were soon fighting raging battles against Assad loyalists. But while violence developed, a deep appreciation of the power of our non-violence remained implanted in our collective psyche.

Once the idea of non-violence became part of our political awareness, the narratives of terrorist groups took a serious hit—they had preached violent resistance for decades, but it was non-violent resistance, sparked by Bouazizi's act of self-immolation, that eventually worked. Islamist extremism was dealt another blow in May 2011, when the United States finally tracked down and killed Osama Bin Laden. It would take a series of exceptionally bloody massacres in 2013 to bring a serious reversal in terrorists' ideological appeal.

We continue to live in awe of and gratitude to the beauty that is 2011. The call of 'the people want the fall of the regime' will be with us our whole lives. In these glorious days, we rediscovered our selfhood and our humanity, and realised that power does not mean violence. We came to see that we matter, that we deserve to live with dignity, and that we were the ones we had been waiting for. Most importantly, we now saw that another future was possible. The light we saw in 2011 continues to inhabit our hearts and guided us in the darkness that was to follow.

Autocracy Strikes Back

When we talk about the nature of the struggle, the true battle is over narratives of legitimacy—the uprisings were themselves the culmination of a prolonged legitimacy crisis. The region's dictatorships had jumped from one narrative of legitimacy to another in an effort to extend their rule, and in 2011, one after another, they ran out of lies.

But broken social contracts aren't like your everyday lies. Social contracts are the very foundation of the ruler's mandate to rule—even for dictators. When a social contract breaks and a dictator loses legitimacy, he's taken an off-ramp onto a one-way road towards collapse. That road may be long or short, but there's no way back, and the destination is a foregone conclusion.

This mass delegitimisation of tyrants was one of the biggest accomplishments of 2011; we exposed their lies once and for all. For all their attempts to pull another lie, they have failed, and they now lie exposed. In coming chapters, we'll be looking at how they tried—unsuccessfully, but also brutally—to sell us new lies.

Delegitimisation is deeply disruptive and results in destabilisation. The wave of revolutions brought down some of the most important, perennial pillars of the old order—Mubarak, Gaddafi, Ben Ali, and Saleh had been in power for a combined total of 128 years. Meanwhile in Syria, the Assad regime was reduced from a major regional power to an entity with curtailed sovereignty, entirely dependent on foreign saviours for its survival.

While most of the regimes managed to survive the events of 2011–2013, the Arab regional order was shaken so severely that, despite the best efforts of our dictators, it has remained volatile and unstable ever since. Some may argue, quite correctly, that what came after this serious destabilisation did not lead to peace and prosperity—we're more acutely aware of that than most, as people living the effects of the continued instability. But allow us to offer another perspective. As fraught as our situation is—while we don't know how long this fight will last, or how many victories and setbacks lie ahead—it's still progress when we're fighting, rather than lying completely subdued.

The regimes' initial shock gave way to fear and hatred. They were forced to acknowledge that the status quo is untenable, even as they floundered in their attempts to fix it. As the turmoil became a fight for their survival, the dictators' contempt for the masses reached new levels, their continued hysteria driven by knowledge of their own insecurity.

By 2013 it was clear what path the elites had chosen. We were about to see the order of autocracy strike back with a vengeance. Our most repressive years were not, in fact, behind us.

Every month following January 2011 was turbulent, but then, in a single week in August 2013, enough blood was spilled to firmly set the region into a downward spiral of violence. On the morning of 14 August, the Egyptian regime committed a massacre in Cairo's Rabaa Square, killing at least 817 civilians, supporters of the ousted Muslim Brotherhood president Mohamed Morsi. Exactly a week later, on 21 August, the Assad regime struck two rebel-held suburbs of Damascus with sarin-filled rockets, killing over a thousand civilians within hours.

Millions experienced that week like a slow-motion train wreck. Our Arab Spring was about to turn into a jihadist Disneyland.

An axis of Arab dictatorships absorbed the initial shock, then fought back against the revolutions with a vengeance. Their goal was to remain in power at any cost—democracy, or any progress towards it, was an existential threat. In fighting to re-establish their control, they conspired with a number of counter-revolutionary forces to abort democratic transitions, increase partisanship, and worsen existing conflicts into open civil wars.

It seemed that these powers were willing to send the entire region to hell if it meant securing their own grasp on power. The first clue to their alliance was in 2011, when Saudi Arabia and its Gulf allies sent troops into Bahrain to help its regime to crush a non-violent uprising. In 2012 and 2013, their influence hastened the militarisation of Syria's uprising. But their most blatant move was when, in the summer of 2013, they bankrolled the overthrow of the elected government in Egypt through a military coup. Their meddling would continue, as they went on to play a destructive role in the civil wars in Libya and Yemen, and even nearly caused a transitional crisis in Tunisia.

It was an all-out war against change, and a scramble to silence all who had once called for it. Iyad too was soon a victim of that wave—he was jailed and then expelled from the UAE for poking fun at tyrants and promoting democracy on Twitter. As the Arab axis of autocracy violently fought back, and as the Arab activists who had inspired the world a few years earlier found themselves targeted, Western governments balked, unable to act decisively to help. The deepening chaos only further empowered the counter-revolution—Arab dictators portrayed themselves as the best safeguard against 'chaos', and even as its antidote. 'We'll become like Syria,' was a line used by almost every regional dictatorship in response to protests or challenge. But it wasn't just a caution—it was a threat.

4

RISE OF THE AXIS

Most discussions about the counter-revolutionary axis start the story in 2013, with the 3 July military coup that toppled Mohamed Morsi, abruptly ending Egypt's democratic transition. This is understandable, given that this was the point when the axis struck, making itself known and its intentions clear. But to truly understand the counter-revolutionary axis (which is also frequently called the 'axis of Arab autocracy'), we have to start in 2011.

In the last chapter we spoke about how we, as citizen activists, experienced 2011. It was rapture and renaissance and rebirth, the coming of age of a new generation. It was as if the Middle East's history was on pause, and then God pressed the 'play' button. Never since 1967 did the region's collective psyche evolve so quickly—but this time, it moved in the opposite direction to after the *Naksa*. Dignity had been beaten out of us and we seemed to have recovered all of it in a few weeks. A new citizen was born, one who broke a formidable barrier of fear to take on their own security forces, head held high.

Most of you reading this are citizens yourselves and will relate to the experiences of the citizen. But consider, for once, how an autocratic ruler who has enjoyed unchecked power and near total impunity for decades would have experienced these same events. It was, for them, sheer terror. They were living a thousand of their worst nightmares every day. The people whom they had robbed and tormented for generations were now on the streets taunting them. They were no longer afraid. They weren't backing down. They were marching through the streets, tearing down their leaders' pictures and knocking down their statues, chanting: 'The people want the fall of the regime.'

Our moment of greatest pride was thus the tyrants' moment of absolute terror. It was then, at the height of our euphoria, that the counter-revolution was born.

We saw the first glimpses of an alliance of dictatorships banding together against the uprisings as early as March 2011, when the Peninsula Shield Force, the GCC's version of NATO, was deployed in response to the largely unarmed uprising in Bahrain. The country of 1.2 million residents had seen over 100,000 protesters (possibly as many as 300,000) rise up to demand democratic reforms.

The commander of the Peninsula Shield Force at the time said that the forces were there to 'bring goodness, peace, and love'.[1] Within hours, the Bahraini government declared a state of emergency, before thousands of security officers backed by tanks and helicopters stormed the protest camp at Pearl Roundabout, brutalising hundreds of protesters and killing four.

Foreshadowing later actions of the Assad regime, the government in Bahrain fomented intentional sectarianisation of Sunnis and Shia who coexisted in the country. A security crackdown soon followed, in which the country's leading opposition figures were imprisoned.

But for months after the Bahrain deployment, it seemed to many of us that the rapidly unrolling protests across the region outstripped the ability of the dictators to predict or respond in a strategically coordinated way; many of these dictators, we thought, had their own feuds and disputes that limited their ability to effectively collaborate. There was a sense of historical inevitability that we the people would triumph, that our victory was within grasp.

This would prove to be naive. While many regional tyrants were fighting for survival, two particular dictatorships were planning ahead. In a private meeting years later, journalist Jamal Khashoggi would tell Iyad of the moment in 2011 when Bandar bin Sultan, secretary general of Saudi Arabia's National Security Council, Khaled al-Tuwaijri, chief of the Royal Court, and the UAE's Mohammad bin Zayed convinced a reluctant King Abdullah to go long. The goal was not only to reverse the Arab Spring and erase its memory, but to create a world in which an Arab Spring was impossible.

* * *

Murmurs of a counter-revolution were first felt in Egypt in 2012, where a protest movement called Tamarod became active; their target was the newly elected administration of President Morsi, who many Egyptians, including 2011 protesters, felt was incompetent, polarising, and partisan. It soon emerged that Tamarod's leadership were receiving funds from the UAE.[2] Meanwhile, popular TV stations owned by wealthy Egyptian businessmen feuded with Brotherhood-friendly ones. The revolutionary camp had been split and the country had become deeply polarised.

The axis proceeded with a then little-known modus operandi that would soon grow to become immediately recognisable across the world. Social media spaces would be flooded with polarising information—much of it false. Societies that had just emerged from decades of crushing tyranny were already fragile; rather than being able to heal, they got concentrated disinformation campaigns by vicious, hysterical autocrats hell-bent on dividing society to foil transitions to democracy.

On 30 June 2013, grievances against Morsi's administration came to a boiling point, and large-scale protests erupted across the country demanding that Morsi step down. It didn't take long, however, for us to see that these were more than mere protests; within forty-eight hours, the Egyptian army intervened with an ultimatum, and two days later they became a military coup.

It soon became clear that the target was not just the Muslim Brotherhood—it was more or less everyone. A counter-revolutionary tsunami hit the country, wreaking blind revenge against all who contributed to the 2011 uprising: protest leaders, politicians, NGOs, independent news outlets, journalists, human rights activists—everyone. The choice was brutally simple—shut up, or face our wrath.

We saw this clampdown beyond Egypt, too. Iyad was then living in the UAE, already a prominent political activist and social media campaigner, with strong relations and ongoing projects with many who were facing arrest in Egypt. By January 2014, it had become clear that he would be next. On 29 April 2014, he received the shocking news that his friend and colleague Bassem Sabry, an Egyptian intellectual and political activist with whom he had founded an activist forum, had fallen to his death from a building in Cairo. The next morning, Iyad was arrested in the UAE and handed expulsion orders. As a stateless Palestinian, he was first deported to Malaysia, before eventually securing a visa to Norway and applying for asylum.

By the time Iyad arrived in Norway and took the stage at the 2014 Oslo Freedom Forum, the world around us had already changed. Earlier in the year, an emboldened Putin had invaded Ukraine. The war in Syria raged on and had displaced millions of Syrians, desperate refugees increasingly taking boats across the Mediterranean to seek safety in Europe. But most significantly, over the summer, ISIS militias had swept across north Syria and Iraq, taking over large areas and declaring a 'caliphate'.

Even in those moments, we saw the counter-revolutionary axis as a graver threat than ISIS. 'It's very important to note that terrorist groups like ISIS present no existential threat to the Arab dictators,' wrote Iyad.[3] In fact, their presence was incredibly convenient, providing an opportunity for the autocrats to present themselves as fighters of terrorism and a force for stability. Even figures as brutal as Syria's Assad and Russia's Putin could now claim to be responsible statesmen who were doing the world a favour by fighting ISIS.

We had moved into the streets and then got stuck in the streets. And we were stuck there long enough to allow the dictators to stage a comeback. A conspiracy was being planned. It had become quite fashionable in many Arab state media to refer to the Arab Spring as a foreign conspiracy, but the real conspiracy was one at home to stop democracy at any price. There was now an organised assault by a counter-revolutionary axis more afraid of the rise of an Arab democracy than the rise of a thousand terror groups—especially of, the rise of a native democracy movement that could capture the imagination of their own youth.

Once again, the Middle East became a playground for tyrants and terrorists. The world went back to its usual cynicism about our region and its future. Once again, we were thought of as refugees and terrorists, when a year earlier we were talked about as protesters and revolutionaries. In our countries, a threatening new social contract was being offered to us, without promising anything back: 'Shut up and trust the strongman with your future, or face our wrath'.

The axis knew, however, that they needed to do better than to offer the region's citizens more sectarianism, demagoguery, jingoism, and repression. They had tried to build a cult of personality around Egypt's Sisi, but despite the efforts of their best propagandists, Sisi lacked charisma and could not appeal to the youth or represent a break with the past. To stem the democratic revolutions, they needed to present a new vision and face, and fast: someone who, they could argue to the world, represented something better than what the Arab Spring had offered.

That figure was Mohammad bin Salman.

MBS: Embodiment of the Axis

There are two reasons why Mohammad bin Salman exemplifies the counter-revolution. The first is that he was the Axis's answer to the Arab Spring, the second that his rise to power since 2015 is a history of the counter-revolution's heyday, peak, and decline. By studying his career so far, we can therefore understand the counter-revolution.

First, however, it's useful to talk about the special post-2011 relationship between Saudi Arabia and the UAE, and why these two countries formed the core of the counter-revolution. Unlike other countries in the region, in 2011 Saudi Arabia and the UAE were uniquely positioned to launch an assault on the revolutions, both enjoying vast wealth and a close alliance with the Western world. Western support meant that they did not face imminent existential external threats, while the lack of a coherent opposition in both countries meant no serious internal threats.

The UAE and Saudi Arabia are not alike, however; Jamal Khashoggi once commented on the difference between them by simply saying, 'Saudi Arabia is not a city state'. Moreover, the two countries actually have a fraught history. In a leaked email from 2017, the UAE's ambassador to the US, Yousef Otaiba, said, 'Abu Dhabi fought 200 years of wars with Saudi over Wahhabism. We have more bad history with Saudi than anyone.'[4]

These two Gulf states do not enjoy a balanced relationship between equals, but a relationship in which the UAE instrumentalises its larger and more powerful neighbour, taking advantage of Saudi family politics. In 2015, former Saudi crown prince

Mohammad bin Nayef warned of Emirati interference in Saudi affairs, alluding to a 'dangerous conspiracy' by the UAE to coopt the Kingdom's royal court politics and install a friendly figure.

Out of the three people who, according to Jamal Khashoggi, convinced King Abdullah to pursue an aggressive counter-revolutionary agenda, one resigned and disappeared from public life, and another found himself imprisoned and purged during the 2017 'Ritz-Carlton incident'. The third is Mohammad bin Zayed (MBZ), Mohammad bin Salman's mentor and the UAE's de facto ruler.

The UAE is a country of 10 million people, of whom only 1 million are citizens. A small native population allows the country to keep its citizens wealthy, but also means that the UAE cannot field an army nearly large enough to contend with regional rivals. The UAE knew that it needed a pliable larger country that could back its regional agenda. This way, not only would the Kingdom's massive resources help MBZ achieve his dark vision for the region—it would also be Saudi Arabia that would bear the brunt of any potential backlash to their actions.

* * *

When he appeared on the world stage, MBS seemed to be a fresh face, allowing him to build a brand without the baggage of a personal or political history. MBS was to be a new kind of Arab ruler, one who would represent a break with the past, pursue a bold campaign of reform and modernisation, and bring peace and stability to his country and region.

In reality, by 2015 the Axis had succeeded in reversing the gains of the revolutions but knew their victory was unsustainable unless they could create a new stability. They needed to present a new contract to the world, and MBS was the man for the job. To the West, it was as though he was saying: 'I'm opening my country culturally and economically, fighting terrorism and extremism, and presenting you all with profit opportunities.'

MBS embodied an attempt to hack the Western mind; his initial success owed as much to latent Western racism as it did to the Axis's own unaccountable brutality and exorbitant wealth. A certain strand of Western thought has always seen us, the people of the Middle East, as somehow lesser on the ladder of humanity. We are hence unworthy of self-rule, certainly of democracy, and the only thing that can work to bring us savages into the civilised world is an enlightened, Western-friendly autocrat who's willing to move fast and break things.

In November 2017, a mere two weeks after the infamous Ritz-Carlton 'anti-corruption' purge—during which MBS's regime detained hundreds of Saudi princes and businessmen in order to seize billions of dollars of assets—American journalist Thomas Friedman wrote a gushing feature in *The New York Times* hailing the crown prince's rise as the arrival of 'Saudi Arabia's Arab Spring, at Last'.[5] His response to criticism for the piece was, quite literally, 'Fuck that'.[6]

For us, the message was clear. We were not only fighting the decades of accumulated wealth and guns of the Saudis and Emiratis—we were also up against ensconced racist Western attitudes about who we are as a people and what we deserve to have, or even aim for, in terms of governance, dignity, and human rights. We knew this, and we knew that we had to do whatever we could to destroy the idol in the Western mind of the benevolent reformer-autocrat. It had already been destroyed in the Middle Eastern mind.

We would end up receiving great help in achieving that goal, from none other than MBS himself.

The Arab Neocons

Rising to power in 2015, MBS quickly branded himself the 'prince of decisiveness'. Within months, and amid great nationalistic fanfare, Saudi Arabia launched the war on Yemen, 'Operation Decisive Storm'. The campaign was supposed to send a message that a new kind of ruler had arrived, who decisively used his Western-supplied superior weapons to establish deterrence vis-a-vis regional rivals such as Iran, as well as extremist groups, and who did not shy away from using military force to accomplish objectives that could be sold to the world in 'war on terror' terms. It was also a dig at Obama, whom the Axis saw as insufficiently supportive of traditional US allies in the region— the message was, we won't wait for you to act to support our interests; we will act ourselves. In addition to the war, ambitious plans were declared to form an 'Islamic NATO', which would in reality be an Axis-led 'coalition of the willing'; these plans were promoted heavily in local media, but never materialised.

The war was supposed to be a decisive blow that would last only a few weeks. When a quick end to the war did not arrive, the Saudi government declared mission accomplished on 'Decisive Storm' and rebranded the war 'Operation Restore Hope'.

The biggest neocon-style move would not take place until after Trump's arrival in the White House. In June 2017, shortly after Trump concluded a visit to Riyadh, where he was received lavishly, Saudi Arabia and the UAE launched a coordinated campaign of disinformation against Qatar, before declaring a complete blockade of the country. Alternative Qatari leaders were promoted on Saudi and Emarati media whilst critical Qatari media infrastructures were hacked.

The Qatari government would later accuse Saudi Arabia and the UAE of attempting not just a blockade, but regime change.[7] Qatar appealed to Turkey to station troops in the country, complicating the strategic situation in the region but also staving off any potential military intervention. The situation was escalated by the expulsion of all Qatari citizens from Axis countries, and by orders from the Axis that its own citizens in Qatar immediately return.

MBS and MBZ behind him represent the new face of autocracy. They brand themselves as visionary reformists—moderate, tolerant, and Western-friendly—and seek to institute political, social, and religious reform through decisive military action.

The Clampdown on Free Speech

The counter-revolution has been marked by a ferocious and unyielding hostility towards free speech and press freedom, and a desire to either dominate or destroy any available public sphere. Some of MBS's most shocking actions stem directly from a burning desire to shut down avenues for free expression. The top demand by the Axis during the June 2017 Qatar crisis was the shutdown of Al Jazeera, the Arabic-speaking world's biggest news network.[8] Arrests of Saudi public intellectuals in September 2017 and of the country's leading women's rights activists in May 2018 targeted especially those with large social media followings.[9] The April 2018 hack of Jeff Bezos's phone, the murder of Khashoggi in October 2018, and the subsequent disinformation campaigns targeting *The Washington Post* were all about free speech.[10]

There is a reason behind this. Regimes that found themselves forced into battles over legitimacy wish to control the public spheres over which these battles are waged.

Before the rise of MBS, Saudi Arabia's public sphere had undergone a breathtaking transformation, thanks to the popularity of social media platforms, especially Twitter. Between 2011 and 2016, Twitter rose in prominence and popularity in the Arab world, quickly becoming a premier hangout of intellectuals and young people. So central was Twitter to the new Arab public sphere that it has been called 'The Parliament of the Arabs'.[11] While regional dictatorships could censor blogs and websites, blocking access to Twitter was seen as economically and politically counterproductive. Arresting Twitter users was similarly costly, and although it did happen, it didn't occur at a scale that caused serious disruption during the Arab Spring's heyday.

The tide turned in 2014, when regional dictatorships went on a counter-offensive that aimed at dominating this online space. The campaign to take over Twitter started in earnest in Egypt, the UAE, and Bahrain, and by 2015 had largely succeeded. The platform became another battleground between Arab citizens and their dictators, with the regimes treating hashtags like they treat demonstrations, sending in the online equivalent of riot police to break them up. Meanwhile, the Saudi online public sphere continued to thrive, due to the large and youthful Saudi Twitter population, and to a still-tolerant political atmosphere.

This changed with the rise of MBS. Twitter's immense popularity and importance in the country led to an apparent decision on the part of the crown prince and his close advisers to conquer Arabic-language Twitter and turn it from a space of public debate by Arab citizens, into a tool of propaganda, repression, and social control.

The Qatar crisis presented another opportunity for MBS to silence dissent, and so he launched a campaign to completely dominate the Saudi public sphere. Soon after the Qatar crisis, the expression of any opinions that called into question the government's action was criminalised, and any kind of support or solidarity with the Qataris was considered outright treason. In August 2017, Saud al-Qahtani, MBS's right-hand man, called for Saudis to rat out any such infringements under the hashtag #TheBlacklist.[12] A few weeks later, a coordinated campaign of arrests targeted over 100 Saudi intellectuals and thought leaders, each of whom had important social capital as an opinion maker in society.[13] A number of charges were brought against the accused, ranging from treason to extremism to abusing social media for nefarious purposes.

By the end of 2017, this conquest was complete, and Arabic Twitter had become a swamp presided over by a handful of government-appointed 'troll masters'. Prominent independent tweeters were in jail, in exile, or intimidated into silence. Others were coerced to join the government's propaganda campaigns. The few remaining outspoken voices—all living outside the Arab world—were harassed, mobbed, and threatened.

Perception Is More Important Than Reality

Along with power consolidation, chauvinistic militarism, and suppression of free speech, the MBS era saw the rise of a new kind of government branding strategy, more reminiscent of glitzy Western commercial PR campaigns than of the usual wooden twentieth-century authoritarian propaganda.

The Axis knew that MBS was about more than just Saudi Arabia—he was the new face of Arab autocracy, and proof in the flesh of the mythical 'benevolent autocrat'. These regimes knew that they were waging a battle over narratives of legitimacy both regionally and globally—a battle that by its very nature would be fought over media rather than on any battlefield. They were aware, in other words, of their own vulnerability to bad press.

Perhaps the best demonstration of this was the 2016 announcement of MBS's new vision for Saudi Arabia, dubbed 'Vision 2030', which came with much pomp and fanfare, bold targets for economic and social development, and flashy videos and infographics. But Vision 2030 had a problem: When it was declared in 2016, the Saudi public sphere was still dynamic enough that a debate kicked off about its targets and feasibility. One prominent Saudi economist in particular was outspoken: Essam al-Zamel boasted large audiences on Twitter and Snapchat, and in a series of videos and tweets explained why the economic portion of the vision was unworkable.

This also meant that the Saudi intellectuals, bloggers, journalists, human rights activists, and women's rights campaigners targeted by MBS's purges weren't just unfortunate collateral damage in a high-stakes battle between rival princes. As opinion makers and social leaders, they were, and still are, at the centre of the story.

That said, being intellectually vacuous, our autocrats don't have enough substance to actually engage in such a battle for ideas with anything approaching normal rules of engagement. Our dictators had only two tools—brutality and money. They set out into the world, including the Western world, with the assumption that everything can be bought. To their credit, Western journalistic traditions cannot be bought; but their PR firms certainly can be.

We choose here to refer to the exercise as PR, rather than propaganda, mainly to call out the role of Western PR firms who help non-Western autocrats to polish their image, in return for millions. That these firms are considered not just legitimate but respectable is to us an interesting facet of Western neo-colonialism. Wealth stolen from us by our dictators lines Western pockets and creates Western jobs in order to polish the image of those same brutal Western-friendly, Western-armed dictators.

The peak moment for MBS's global prestige was his visit to the United States in March 2018. MBS was given a hero's welcome, not only by Trump administration officials, but also reportedly by the likes of Oprah Winfrey, Dwayne 'The Rock' Johnson, Bill Clinton, John Kerry, Michael Bloomberg, Bill Gates, Jeffrey Goldberg, Tim Cook, Elon Musk, Peter Thiel, Richard Branson, Bob Iger, Satya Nadella, and Jeff Bezos.[14]

MBS's charm offensive was carefully targeted. He thought that if he had enough celebrities and influencers behind him, this would guarantee him an airtight reputation and the impunity to do anything. Behind this was a belief that PR was more powerful than reality, and that with the right branding and marketing, any perception can be upheld, regardless of the underlying truths. This was also quite convenient—changing realities is hard, but all PR campaigns need is money, and he has a lot of it. MBS didn't have to actually be a reformer; he could use his wealth to buy a reformer's brand.

The new face of Arab autocracy was very popular indeed. When the crown prince's interview with CBS's *60 Minutes* was broadcast, enough white folks were taken by his charm that even fellow human rights activists were arguing to us that we needed to 'give him a chance'. At that point, MBS had already launched a destructive war on Yemen, doubled down on support for regional dictatorships in Egypt and Bahrain, launched a regime change attempt on Qatar, arrested dozens of Saudi intellectuals, and destroyed the Arab public sphere on Twitter.

Yet we knew that when dictators are treated as heroes internationally, they do not become any less dictatorial. They see their global popularity as conferring legitimacy, and they only get more emboldened. Within weeks of his triumphant return to Saudi Arabia, we were already receiving troubling reports that MBS was about to move in on the last group of Saudi activists not yet in prison: the women's rights activists.

Repression of the Women's Rights Movement

Saudi Arabia has an almost comically terrible record on women's rights, as great strides since the mid-twentieth century in education have not been matched by increased women's autonomy. In the 1950s, female literacy in Saudi Arabia was in the single digits, while by the 2010s, young Saudi women were almost universally educated—in fact, Saudi women are today some of the best educated in the region. But social and legal norms did not keep pace, and women in Saudi Arabia continued to be treated as wards who must permanently be placed under the protection of a male guardian. As Saudi Arabia became wealthier and its regime more powerful, successive administrations only doubled down on these repressive norms, justifying them as reflecting the unique tradition and religious interpretation of the Wahhabi establishment, which the ruling family leans on for additional legitimacy.

As a consequence of living in one of the most patriarchal countries on earth, Saudi society developed some of the world's most courageous and resilient women's rights movements. The country's first acts of defiance against the women's driving ban go back to the early 1990s; nearly thirty years later, the movement had become a real force in the Saudi social debate. Encouraged by the region's age of resistance after 2011, Saudi women openly defied the driving ban in 2012, and again in 2014. Saudi women's rights activists quickly became among the most prominent stars of the Saudi public sphere.

We knew that MBS would not tolerate any activism that does not proceed from the state. We also knew that these women were too smart and principled to enter into a Faustian pact with MBS. More importantly, we knew that MBS could not move against the Saudi women's rights movement without causing serious damage to his image as a reformer before the world. After all, he could justify his roundup of Saudi intellectuals by calling them 'extremists', and he could justify his roundup of elites and princes by calling them 'corrupt'. There simply was no way to justify to the world a roundup of Saudi feminists.

Yet MBS was so strengthened by his March 2018 tour of the US that he felt that his PR was invincible. The clampdown on women's rights activists came in May. The most important figures of the Saudi feminist movement were arrested in midnight raids, while government PR networks plastered their faces on 'wanted' posters and accused them of treason. The women later reported being subjected to horrific torture, including whippings, electric shock, and sexual harassment.[15]

Initially buoyed by a largely uncritical Western attitude towards the new face of Arab autocracy, Saudi PR efforts quickly descended into farce. When Canada's foreign minister protested the treatment of Saudi women's rights activists, MBS's response was all but unhinged. In a series of moves redolent of the Qatar blockade a year earlier, he severed relations with Canada and ordered all Saudis in Canada to immediately return home, including students and patients.[16] At the same time, his government's PR outlets pumped out vague threats and ridiculous content about Canada's own human rights record.[17]

Fighting Our Enemy

Since 2011, the governments of Saudi Arabia and the UAE have deployed their significant financial resources—and leveraged their relationship with the West—to stop democracy at any price, out of fear that it might reach their own doorstep. They helped to crush Bahrain's uprising; bankrolled a return to military dictatorship in Egypt; armed a rogue military leader in Libya; and mismanaged a democratic transition in Yemen before launching a destructive war there.[18]

By late 2018, despite the problems the Axis had run into on several of these operations, there was a sense that they were winning. Then, on 2 October 2018, Jamal Khashoggi stepped into the Saudi consulate in Istanbul. Within a few weeks, everything would change. While the Axis ended the year vicious, wealthy, and powerful, the narratives of legitimacy it relied upon had taken a very serious hit.

There are good enemies and bad enemies. With good enemies, their enmity actually proves your narratives and increases your legitimacy. With bad enemies, their enmity hurts your narratives and strips away your legitimacy.

Given our open enmity towards MBS, some may think that the longer he stays in power, the more he's 'winning' and the more we're 'losing'.

But MBS is a great enemy for us to have. He's an excellent sledgehammer to the regional order. He is also single-handedly making our argument for us—that dictators cannot bring stability or prosperity; that Western support for dictatorship is unconscionable and strategically damaging; and that a world order in which dictators are empowered produces boundless human misery. That leaves us to make the next argument—that the Middle East, indeed the world, will continue to be a crisis factory until the grand intergenerational project that began in 2011 is completed, with a democratic transition across the region, an end to tyranny, and an end to international support for dictators.

Should MBS step away from power, a thousand knives will be waiting for him. It is a mistake to view this narrow battle as the war; this, as we have repeated, is a thirty-year project, an intergenerational transition. MBS is an embodiment of Arab tyranny in its final stage: brutal, hysterical, paranoid, stupid, running for one ideological cover after another, raining money here and there to look for allies or friends. But ultimately, MBS is damned whatever he does. He may well succeed in repressing us, but our movement wins either way. Even if we lose, we win. Even if he wins, he loses.

Our demand is huge: the transition of a region of half a billion people to democracy, denied to us by colonialism, the ugly forces that were unleashed to battle it, and the neo-colonial system that came in its stead. Ours is a project not only to knock out dictators and build democratic states, but also to upturn a world order that has empowered dictators and denied us freedom. It would be great for such a transition to happen without torture dungeons, without murdered journalists, without civil wars or refugee waves. But we don't live in that kind of world, and our regimes would rather burn the region to the ground than countenance our democracy and freedom.

While our focus in this book is on the counter-revolutionary axis led by Saudi Arabia and the UAE, this is by no means the only counter-revolutionary coalition that has stood against the march of democracy in the region. Notably, the Iranian regime and its satellites have also expended extensive resources to fight back against uprisings, not only within Iran itself but also in Syria, and more recently in Iraq and Lebanon.

We focus on the Arab-led axis for two key reasons. First, the Saudi–UAE axis is led by Sunni Arab regimes whose cultural commonalities with the majority of the Arabic-speaking world makes them particularly insidious; they can run influential operations anywhere from Morocco to Iraq. Second, unlike Iran, the Saudi and Emirati regimes have massive financial resources and enjoy close relations with the West, which is why they have faced little to no pushback despite their destructive interventions, making them particularly effective.

While we believe both of these counter-revolutionary coalitions are existential threats to freedom in the region, only the Saudi–UAE axis can effectively prevent a critical mass of democratic transitions that would tip the regional scale. Out of the two, the centre of gravity of the Middle East's tyranny is Riyadh, without which the UAE would lie exposed. The Saudi regime is the most serious bulwark against our freedom, and so long as it is empowered, no revolution in the region is safe. In the struggles for freedom in Bahrain, Yemen, Egypt, and Sudan, the people's persecutors are reliant on support from Riyadh, and some firepower must be reserved for its regime. This means that every Saudi voice for freedom immediately becomes our ally; their struggle is our struggle, their pain our pain, their victory our victory.

MBS peaked with his tour of America in March 2018, before shooting himself in the foot with the arrests of women's rights activists, then stabbing himself with a poisoned knife with the Khashoggi murder. The epicentre of Arab tyranny is wounded and poisoned.

It is dangerous for tyrants to rule by force alone; such tyranny is fierce but fragile. After our dictators' social contract broke in 2011, they tried to put a new offer on the table in 2014, mistaking a hollow PR campaign for a contract. They now rule solely by naked force and repression, having lost all claim to legitimacy.

It is worth noting that even while MBS's prestige took a nosedive, the UAE stuck by him. This was not out of confidence, but out of strategic rigor mortis—there is no plan B beyond MBS. Arab autocracy is running out of options. The tyrants' time is up.

PART II

HORIZONS

5

THE VITALS

So far, we have given a narrative account of the history of legitimacy in our region. Now we will examine the region's future horizons. We want to start by taking a look at the data scorecard—the vitals that back up, confirm, and punctuate the picture till now. Above all, these statistics show a clear divide between our regimes and our societies, and trends that carry across most of the region's countries.

In Chapter 1, we explored the modern history of the region as a series of broken social contracts. Post-colonial Arab regimes derived their legitimacy from the struggle for independence from Western hegemony. They promised Arab unity and dignity, but only delivered defeat, humiliation, and internecine conflict. After the oil boom, Arab regimes promised to lift the masses out of poverty and illiteracy, but they coupled that with a complete expropriation of political rights. Faced with a crisis of legitimacy, they seized upon the opportunity presented by the US 'war on terror', adopting the fight against terrorism as a new pillar of their international and domestic legitimacy.

What has been the consequence of this dismal track record, and what is the current state of the Arab regional order?

Let's look now at the vitals—theirs, and ours.

Economics

We'll start with economic performance. The Arab region is one of the most youthful regions in the world—60 per cent of the population is under the age of thirty.[1] A total of 108 million Arabs are currently transitioning into adulthood—the highest such number in the region's history. Yet our region leads the world in youth unemployment, in a trend seen across its countries, including oil-rich Gulf states. In 2018, the Middle East's youth unemployment rate stood at 30 per cent, more than twice the world's average of 14 per cent. Among women, the situation is worse, with 50 per cent unemployment compared to a global average of 16 per cent.[2] In 2016, *The Economist* summarised the situation: 'Elsewhere, a large youthful population would be regarded as an economic blessing. But in the Arab world the young are treated, for the most part, as a curse, to be suppressed.'[3] Youth should be the Arab world's primary resource. But faced with oppression and a lack of opportunities, many of our young people are wasting away.

In 2010, it was estimated that Arab countries needed to create a hundred million jobs in order to remain economically sustainable—this did not happen. In 2018, 35 per cent of youth in Arab countries regarded unemployment as the region's single biggest obstacle, and 70 per cent thought governments were not doing enough to address it.[4]

Arab economies remain stunted. When one puts together the Arab states' economic output, including in the fossil fuel industry, we end up with a total GDP equivalent only to the economy of Japan, which has a third of their aggregate population.[5]

What are Arab economies producing? Even in countries that are supposed to be agricultural powerhouses, the top export is still oil. For Saudi Arabia, 63 per cent of the country's exports are in crude petroleum, and 9 per cent in refined petroleum. Petroleum gas, crude petroleum and refined petroleum together make up more than 94 per cent of Algeria's exports, and 23 per cent of Egypt's exports.[6] Meanwhile, a tiny proportion of manufactured exports are in high technology. It is no wonder that we lead the world in youth unemployment—instead of creating products that the world needs, our economic model seems to be based upon digging holes in the ground.

The agricultural field is still structurally important—in 2020, it provided 15 per cent of all jobs.[7] But even here, we are faced with a dangerous unsustainability; not only is the Arab region one of the most water-stressed in the world, but it is projected that it will be one of the worst hit by rising temperatures due to climate change.

The state of the region's economies, in addition to rampant political repression, has contributed to a worsening brain drain. A large number of the MENA's highly qualified native experts are working abroad in developed countries, most of them never returning home. This trend has been exacerbated in the aftermath of the Arab Spring and subsequent refugee crisis. In the 2019–2020 Arab Opinion Index, 22 per cent of citizens across the Arab world said that they wanted to emigrate.[8]

What about imports? Disturbingly, the MENA region is the world's largest importer of arms.[9] Somehow, our regimes manage to import more weapons than any region in the world without actually winning any wars—except wars that they wage against us, the people.

Should we turn away from economics and look at politics, we're faced with no less stark a picture. Trailing behind the world Democracy Index average of 5.44, in 2019 the Arab region had an average score of 3.35—a figure that hides behind it brutality, repression, prisons, and torture dungeons.[10] The region, on aggregate, also has one of the lowest Press Freedom Indices in the world.[11] The lack of free speech is reflected in a stunted cultural scene and crippled publishing industry. We have a bigger chance of getting published in English than in Arabic; in fact, for many Arabs, writing in English rather than in their native language has become a form of self-censorship. Clamping down on free speech means that bad ideas can't be tackled openly, even as persecution creates grievances that can drive people to extremism.

In 2002, five Arab states were recognised by the UN as being in the midst of serious conflict; that number is now eleven. While the region is only home to 5 per cent of the world's population, a report by the United Nations Development Programme found that in 2014, the Arab world accounted for 45 per cent of the world's terrorism; 68.5 per cent of its battle-related deaths; 47 per cent of its internally displaced; and 57.5 per cent of its refugees.[12] The same report estimated that up to 75 per cent of all Arabs may soon be living in countries vulnerable to conflict.

Our regimes' history of broken promises has caused mass disillusionment. It is important to note that most natives of the Middle East did not disbelieve what was being offered to them, but rather their government's ability to deliver. In the 2019–2020 Arab Opinion Index, 76 per cent of respondents wanted a democratic system of government, and only 17 per cent opposed one (in comparison, a 2020 poll found over 30 per cent supported unelected strongman rule in Romania, Slovakia, Latvia, and Bulgaria—all EU member states).[13] When asked about the 2011 uprisings, 58 per cent of Arab respondents said they were positive developments despite their aftermath; only 28 per cent said they were negative.[14]

Most citizens of the MENA today would still favour closer social and economic integration between countries, including open borders, foreign policy coordination, and common defence; they still largely believe their governments should deliver strong economies; quality health and education; and security and the prevention of terrorism. But these promises seem further away than ever. To many young citizens of the Middle East, the revolutions of 2011 represented a chance for meaningful change, but with their suppression the region was left even more repressive and unstable. It's impossible to disconnect the fact that the Middle East is now a crisis factory from the fact that our regional order is dominated by dictatorships. To be a citizen of the MENA today feels like being on board the *Titanic*, knowing full well that we are headed for an iceberg. We are more than capable of being at the steering wheel, in control of our destiny. But instead, we and our families are locked in cages way below deck.

Is There a Way Out?

At a networking dinner in Copenhagen in 2016, Iyad had a memorable conversation with a chic, white-haired woman, who spoke English with Italian intonation. Iyad had introduced himself as an Arab Spring activist, almost apologetically—by this point, the Arab Spring had turned into a jihadist free-for-all. 'I'll tell you what your problem was,' she said. 'There wasn't enough blood.' Iyad was taken aback, and it probably showed. The daily news from the region was about massacres and battles and bombings. We were knee-deep in blood.

The woman went on, arguing that the historical record did not make one very optimistic about the prospects for successful revolution. The classical revolutions that were successful were uncompromising in their elimination of the old elite. She cited the French and Russian revolutions—'revolutionary justice', as she described it, had to be unapologetically brutal.

Her words stuck, particularly because the general mood at the time among many Arabs was morose, as we conducted postmortems of what had gone wrong. Among the wide range of opinions expressed were suggestions by some that, perhaps, we weren't radical enough. A common understanding of radical change asserts that to uproot a dictatorship, what works is either violent revolution or a foreign invasion.

'Violence alone, violence committed by the people, violence organised and educated by its leaders, makes it possible for the masses to understand social truths and gives the key to them,' wrote Frantz Fanon in *The Wretched of the Earth* in 1961.[15] A couple of centuries before him, Denis Diderot purportedly said: 'Men will never be free until the last king is strangled with the entrails of the last priest.'

The view that the only way to remove a dictatorship is through uncompromising brutality would make you into either a radical revolutionary who excuses wanton violence, or a reactionary conservative who will tolerate any amount of abuse by dictators to avoid wanton violence. This is perhaps why many view 'regime change' as only being supported by desperate radicals with nothing to lose, or traitors happy to ride to victory on a foreign army's tanks. By comparison with these images, engagement with dictators in the hope of getting them to change their brutal behaviour would appear to be responsible and pragmatic.

We've spoken to enough intellectuals, policy makers, and think-tankers to know that this view is prevalent. We've also had enough conversations to know that they truly do care about human rights. Many find dealing with dictatorships genuinely revolting, but view it as a necessary evil, because the alternatives are worse. Nobody wants to be blamed for unleashing a tyrant's worst excesses, or precipitating breakage and instability. But what if this zero-sum view is outdated, reflecting an old paradigm that no longer represents our reality?

Recall the 'vicious triangle' from Chapter 2. Triangles are stable geometric figures; each side relies upon the others for support, and pressure upon any of the sides is distributed onto the other two.

But triangles are susceptible to pressure on the inside. The best way to break the vicious triangle is through a steady but relentless strengthening of society, until it sheds it like old skin. The antithesis of oppressive states is strong societies.

The statistics above are not a reflection of the talents and abilities of the Middle East's individuals, but rather of the cruelty, kleptocracy, and incompetence of its tyrannies. The region's instability and our regimes' track record of failure may obscure the fact that our societies have undergone an impressive evolution over the past few decades. Our revolutions did not come out of a vacuum—they were the result of a social maturation in terms of demographics, education, connectivity, and attitude towards governance. Today's youth are the largest, most educated, most connected, and most urbanised generation in our region's long history.

Demographics

All countries in the world have started from a state of high birth rates and high child mortality, evolving towards low birth rates and low child mortality, often with a baby boom in between. In the Arab world, the average family size has dropped from an average of 6.8 children per woman in 1970–1975 to 2.8 children per woman in 2018.[16] A 2019 study by Yale University found that seven of the world's top fifteen fertility declines have occurred in Arab countries.[17] In fact, birth rates in several countries in the region drop below the 2.1 required to sustain population levels, such as in Lebanon and Bahrain. At the same time, child mortality rates across the region have been dropping steadily.

Demographic maturation is correlated with several key social developments—most importantly, the status of women. While child marriage continues to be a problem that needs to be seriously addressed, across the region the age of first marriage has risen notably for women, who are more likely to delay marriage and childbirth while they pursue education and perhaps a career.[18] Lower birth rates are also associated with a shift in family structure from extended families to nuclear families—smaller family units have a greater chance of moving away from the traditional values of the tribe, especially as more Arabs move from rural settings into cities, in search of better economic opportunities.

Education and Access to Information

The rise in education is perhaps the single most important social transformation across the region. In the mid-twentieth century, when most countries in the region gained their independence, literacy rates were very low, but especially low for women (often, female literacy rates were less than half those of men).

Today, while literacy rates in the MENA remain low among seniors (less than a third of those aged sixty-five and above can read and write), more than 90 per cent of those between the ages of fifteen and twenty-four are literate, with several countries achieving almost universal youth literacy.[19] (Notably, while the Arab region is among the world's most youthful, the median age of its heads of state is sixty-five.) Furthermore, the literacy gap between young men and young women has been all but eliminated. In several countries in the region, more young women are graduating from local colleges than young men—women also regularly score higher grades.[20]

While education alone does not automatically lead to democratisation, there's reason to believe that it fosters movement in that direction. In research investigating the correlation between various countries' average years of schooling in 1970 and the existence of democratic governance in 2015, no countries that had high levels of education fifty years ago failed to become, or failed to remain, democratic.[21]

High literacy on its own would mean little were everyone forced to read from the same book (after all, North Korea is another country with virtually universal literacy). It's significant that, between 2000 and 2013, the number of people with access to the internet in the Middle East grew by over 5,300 per cent. This trend also holds true across the Arab countries of North Africa. In 2020, the internet penetration rate in the region was 70.2 per cent, well above the global average of 58.8 per cent.[22]

Interestingly, a lot of the gain has occurred *after* the Arab Spring. In July 2012, the month-to-month growth of Twitter usage in Saudi Arabia was an astounding 3,000 per cent. Several countries in the region now hold global records in this area—the United Arab Emirates leads the world in smartphone penetration (80.6 per cent) and Saudi Arabia leads the world in Twitter penetration (52 per cent).

The internet has presented a unique opportunity. Not only is this the most literate generation in the region's history, but thanks to the internet, it's also the generation that is most connected, therefore having access to a far more diverse set of views than any generation before it. Predictably, the internet also presents a problem for our dictatorships.

Perceptions and Expectations

There is another noteworthy trend that is far more difficult to quantify: The attitudes of many young people in the region towards their own governments have shifted. Aided by their increased connectivity, the youth are more aware of their rights and their situation than ever before.

Today, through social media, a young girl with internet access in Khartoum, Sudan, can see what life looks like for someone in

Edinburgh, Sacramento, or Sao Paulo. Your attitudes and aspirations change when you are connected to others—both to people who share your plight, and to people who don't. This is especially true for minorities and traditionally marginalised groups, such as women, but it applies to any human being trying to exercise their fundamental rights. The global communications revolution means that they can now see that what they suffer is not inevitable, and that a better life is possible.

In 2010, Egypt conducted a national youth survey which showed that only 16 per cent of those aged eighteen to twenty-nine voted in any elections, and only 2.3 per cent of young people had taken part in volunteer work.[23] When Egypt's cabinet discussed the findings in December 2010, the conversation was about how the country's youth were passive and indifferent. Three months later, Egypt's 'apathetic' youth had successfully toppled Hosni Mubarak.

In a way, the 2011 uprisings were the illustration of a generational gap in political values and aspirations. Most of the protesters were in their twenties, chanting against regimes that had been built before they were even born and accepted by parents whose experiences they didn't share. Even though the uprisings were suppressed, they gave rise to a new citizen and delegitimised the political order.

The last decade in particular has seen a rise in civil society activism, aided by new technology and accelerated by the revolutionary waves that have swept the region and the world. These activists include journalists, bloggers, writers, entrepreneurs, organisers, and political campaigners. Their efforts are key to increasing society's resilience and turning the positive social trends described above into meaningful political change. But they're frequently threatened, and their efforts are constantly thwarted.

To the nearly 60 per cent of people who today live in unfree countries, the communications revolution has been even more transformative than it has been given credit for. In our region, we have a generation that is more literate, more prosperous, and more tuned in to diverse points of view than any generation that preceded it. They are more aware of their own plight, and of the plight of others, than ever before. They are also more able to speak out, to rally, and to scream into the void of the internet. All of this progress brings hope, but with hope also comes pain—especially when that better life is so near, and yet so far.

* * *

The transformation that has taken place across our societies over the past few decades is cause for optimism, but it also brings instability. Even as societies matured, our regimes remained stubbornly opposed to political change—in fact, the trend has been towards more repression. This may seem counterintuitive, but it is expected—dictatorships become more vengeful and paranoid when they're threatened, including when the societies over which they rule grow more dynamic and defiant. It is therefore important to note that while the social transformation described in this chapter is good news, it is not enough to bring about positive change by itself; left to themselves, the dictatorships will become more, not less, tyrannical.

People who live in open societies often underestimate how difficult it is to uproot tyranny once it establishes itself. If it was easy to overthrow deep-seated dictatorships, they wouldn't last very long. Dictators use their power to hollow out society, gut the opposition, buy the best arms and surveillance technology, and hire the best PR consultants, all while ensuring they are useful to the world's hegemonic powers so as to receive special treatment. Once internationally accepted as the sovereign government, they benefit from a global ecosystem that allows them to entrench themselves—and brutalise their people—even further. This is how our tyrants ended up ruling unchallenged for decades, becoming fabulously rich in the process.

Our societies have started running faster than their regimes, but the brutality and intransigence of our dictatorships threaten to reverse the gains we've made. We've seen them assault civil society, constrict the public sphere, attack free speech, fill dungeons with political prisoners, and wage wars on their own people. In the extreme case of Syria, this has resulted in hundreds of thousands of deaths, millions of refugees, and a lost generation. As we stand today, our regimes are a direct danger to the health and prosperity of our societies.

We need to stop believing in regimes and start believing in societies. We will only keep going from tyranny to terrorism to foreign intervention if we don't find our voices and break the cycle from within. And we could use a helping hand—it could make the difference between a trail of tragedies that spans generations, and achieving democracy within our lifetimes.

How do we strengthen our societies while not empowering the vicious triangle of oppression around them? And how do we change the power dynamic, so as to subvert the triangle without hurting the societies within? We believe this is eminently possible, should the political will exist, and should we shed our outdated paradigms. In the next two chapters, we attempt to outline such a strategy.

6

DEALING WITH DICTATORS

In 1999, Iyad met with Rabah, an Iraqi software engineer living in the UAE who was running a local software solutions company. Rabah had moved to Dubai from Baghdad a few years earlier—this was pre-invasion Iraq, a country strangled by sanctions and traumatised by dictatorship, but not yet broken by war, occupation, civil strife, and terrorism. With very limited access to external expertise, Rabah had taught himself programming. While still a university student in 1990s Baghdad, he had developed an Arabic-language computer game, recruiting a development team from the university. An architecture student had become his artist and animator, and a particularly talented oud player (and medical student) had provided the music.

In a conversation centred around a shared passion for computer games development, what stood out at the time was how devastating the effects of the Saddam regime were—and how the sanctions devised to contain Saddam only made things worse for ordinary Iraqis. The regime had isolated the Iraqi people, and the sanctions exacerbated this isolation. Iraqis had virtually no contact with the outside world, no means of communication, and no media that wasn't state-controlled. Satellite TV was banned. There were no mobile phones, and less than 0.1 per cent of Iraqis had access to the internet. Few could travel (Iraq's national airlines were grounded, which meant that travellers had to take land transport to Jordan and fly from Amman). Imported goods and equipment, including books, were very expensive, if they were available at all.

Many years later, we caught up with Maryam Nayeb Yazdi, the award-winning Canadian-Iranian human rights activist quoted in Chapter 2. Maryam had founded Persian2English, a translation portal that was an essential resource for journalists during the 2009 Iranian uprising. Ahmed's discussions with her focused on the Iran nuclear deal, whose aftermath saw the killing, torturing, and silencing of many of Maryam's Iranian comrades. She was against the sanctions imposed on Iran, but also opposed a deal that paid no regard at all to Iran's human rights situation. When the nuclear deal was signed, it eased sanctions, but it also empowered and strengthened a dictatorship. Iran's regime was emboldened to go on a rampage through its support for the Assad regime in Syria and for militant actors across the Middle East, as well as to further persecute Iranian civil society activists. Meanwhile, many of the voices of the 2009 uprising were left wasting away in the Iranian regime's jails, or living in limbo as asylum seekers outside Iran. Few have been able to continue their activism in exile.

Two Failed Models

In our view, Iran and Iraq represent two failed models of how to deal with dictatorial regimes. In Iraq, the West applied policies of muscular containment and sanctions, followed by a disastrous and illegal invasion, after which the country slid into chaos. In Iran, sanctions were also used, followed by a narrow-minded diplomatic deal that strengthened the dictatorship, a few short years after it had brutally crushed a pro-democracy uprising. Both had disastrous effects on the region as a whole. Put on the defensive, other regional dictatorships took the opportunity to inflate narratives of sectarianism and nationalism. A 'vicious triangle' dynamic was re-energised. Resurgent tyranny came with resurgent terrorism, and a new cycle of foreign intervention.

It is about time we realise that blanket sanctions do not bring about regime change—they bring about regime entrenchment. Military intervention doesn't bring democracy—it causes social breakage that leads to lost generations. Uncritical engagement and legitimisation of dictatorships does not cause them to become more moderate but increases their resilience and ability to crush their own people.

How would you tackle an aggressive domestic abuser who has brutalised, traumatised, and isolated his own household? Besieging and starving the house—or worse yet, bombing it—to get rid of the abuser would seem absolutely irresponsible, but so too would treating the abuser as a legitimate father figure, in the hope that he'll start acting more responsibly. Dictatorships should be treated as hostage-takers, and the societies they suppress should be treated as hostages. We should seek to engage these regimes such that we empower society more than we empower the regimes. If we try to pressure or punish the regimes, we should do so without punishing society.

In this chapter and the next, we will offer ideas that follow this line of thinking—first, how to deal with dictatorships, and second, how to deal with societies. To start, let's look at some crucial aspects of what makes dictatorships tick.

A Brief Study of Tyranny

Dictatorial regimes may seem diverse in their tactics, and their behaviour may at times seem erratic and irrational. But at the root they share basic commonalities that can be analysed and understood. Among the most crucial of these is their relationship with corruption. Dictatorship is, above everything else, really good business. When you can control the entire economic output of a society as well as all of its natural resources, you can become fantastically rich faster than any tech entrepreneur or financial speculator.

The richest people in the world today aren't the likes of Jeff Bezos and Bill Gates—who are legally obligated to play by the rules, reveal their wealth, and pay taxes. Far richer are autocrats like Putin, whose wealth has been estimated at $200 billion;[1] and Mohammad bin Salman, whose family reportedly controls $1.4 trillion.[2] The late Libyan dictator Muammar Gaddafi's wealth was estimated to be more than $200 billion, after forty-two years in power.[3] Hosni Mubarak of Egypt, who ruled Egypt for twenty-nine years, reportedly accumulated around $70 billion.[4] Even the late Ali Abdullah Saleh, who ruled the impoverished country of Yemen, is estimated to have amassed $32–60 billion during his thirty-three years in power.[5]

But plunder only tells half the story. Dictatorships normally have stunted economies, and they're rarely good places for long-term investment. To safeguard and multiply their loot, dictators need access to Western economies—they effectively use Western financial markets to launder the money they steal from their own people. The immense financial resources they amass are a crucial contributor to the resilience and persistence of their regimes, allowing them to have well-equipped intelligence and security forces, and to pay for the best Western PR and lobbying firms to maintain their image as 'visionary reformers' and 'responsible allies'.

The interest in Western economies goes beyond using them as financial safe havens or for high-yield investment. While dictators and their inner circle of kleptocrats may turn their own countries into a wasteland, they want to live the high life themselves, with trips to Paris, evenings in New York, and shopping sprees in London. Even as their own educational institutions fall apart, they want their children to attend the best European private schools (North Korean dictator Kim Jong-un was educated at a Swiss boarding school).[6] Even as their own public health sector remains stunted and inefficient, they want to get treatment in private hospitals in the US or the UK.

Facilitating this is an ecosystem of global corruption that includes shell companies, so-called tax havens, and unscrupulous officials. As pointed out by Ilya Zaslavskiy of the Free Russia Foundation, this corruption is propped up by tyrants' shared worldview, which poses that only the elites matter; that everything and everyone is corruptible; and that individual human life does not have any inherent value. Unfortunately, many politicians, lobbyists, and businessmen in the West treat dictators in ways that confirm their beliefs.

Magnitsky's Revenge

Through tackling this ecosystem, it is possible to change the incentive structure within which dictatorships operate. It requires real political will, and an appreciation of the damage, destruction, and instability wrought by these regimes. One of the most successful attempts to do this has been the Magnitsky sanctions.

The Magnitsky sanctions are named after Sergei Magnitsky, a Russian man who was found dead in a Russian prison on 16 November 2009, chained to a bed and lying in a pool of his own urine. He was thirty-seven years old, and a married father of two. Magnitsky wasn't a political dissident, an activist, or a journalist—he was a tax attorney. Two years earlier, he had been hired by Bill Browder, then the head of the largest Western investment firm in Russia, in the aftermath of their offices being raided by the Russian interior ministry on tax evasion charges.

Magnitsky looked into what had happened—and went on to uncover a $230 million corruption scandal in which Russian sovereign authorities—including the interior ministry, police, and judiciary—were implicated. Magnitsky and Browder initially thought they had uncovered a rogue operation, and that if they reported it to the authorities, the good guys would get the bad guys. They went ahead and filed criminal complaints with every law enforcement agency in Russia, including the FSB, the Russian equivalent of the FBI.

At first, it seemed that the case was being taken seriously. But then, in November 2008, Magnitsky was arrested at his home and subjected to a year-long nightmare, as officials tried to coerce him to confess to having falsified the charges, alleging that, far from having uncovered corruption, he had defrauded the government of $230 million on Bill Browder's instructions. Every time he refused to sign a confession, Magnitsky was moved into increasingly harsh conditions in increasingly squalid cells. His health deteriorated, and he developed gallstones and pancreatitis, for which he was denied treatment. A surgery was later approved— but then, shortly before the surgery date, he was moved to another prison lacking the necessary facilities.

By November 2009, he was in constant pain. Fearing that he'd die on their watch, the prison authorities put him in an ambulance and sent him to a prison hospital. Screaming in agony, Magnitsky was kept on a psychiatric ward instead of being offered emergency treatment. Two hours later, he was dead. Prison officials said he died due to a heart attack, but it was later revealed that he had been beaten to death by a group of Russian interior ministry officers.

Sergei Magnitsky had a cruel and undignified death, but little did he know that a piece of legislation named after him would haunt his persecutors for years after his death. 'That morning, I made a vow to Sergei's memory, to his family, and to myself that I would seek justice and create consequences for the people who murdered him,' said Bill Browder. Browder at one point considered Putin to be a patriot, a nationalist leader who was on a quest to rein in corrupt oligarchs. But Magnitsky's ordeal and death uncovered a new reality.

Browder took Magnitsky's story to US senators Benjamin Cardin and John McCain, who proposed a new piece of legislation called the Sergei Magnitsky Rule of Law Accountability Act, which would freeze the assets and ban the visas of Russians involved in serious human rights abuse. In December 2012, the Magnitsky Act was signed into law.

Putin Reacts

The Russian regime lashed out against the Magnitsky Act almost immediately. Scrambling to retaliate, within days of its passage, Putin signed a bill banning Americans from adopting Russian children. The Russian authorities would go on to posthumously convict Sergei Magnitsky of the crimes brought against him, in the first ever trial of a dead person. Russian ex-president Dmitry Medvedev even went on to issue warnings to Browder, who by now had taken it upon himself to convince other countries to pass similar legislation.

Browder had stumbled upon one of the most effective ways to hold dictators to account and make them hurt—targeted sanctions. He had wanted justice for Sergei, but he hadn't anticipated that the Magnitsky Act would elicit such a huge backlash from the Russian regime—the intensity of which signalled that the Act had hit on something extremely valuable.

The Magnitsky Act prevented the Russian regime's elite—most of whom were either fronts for or partners of Putin himself—from enjoying their ill-gotten wealth. Kleptocracy is less rewarding when you aren't able to safeguard your money in foreign bank accounts, use it to buy luxury houses in Western capitals, or support a lavish lifestyle for your family and mistresses abroad. Kleptocrats were now left with the unattractive option of keeping their money back home, where it can't really grow much, and can be stolen back from them the way they stole it from others.

The pain brought by the Magnitsky Act was initially slow, and it was limited to the United States. Meanwhile Europe balked, hoping to maintain an amicable working relationship with Russia. But when Putin invaded Ukraine in 2014, Europe got on board—and that's when things got really serious. Browder has since had success promoting similar legislation in Canada, Estonia, Lithuania, and the United Kingdom.

Hacking an Election—for Sanctions Relief

In 2016, during the run-up to the US presidential elections, the Russian lawyer Natalia Veselnitskaya held discussions with high-ranking Trump campaign officials on 'a program about the adoption of Russian children'.[7] Amid all the hysteria about Russian meddling in the US election, and the allegations of collusion between the Trump campaign and the Russian regime, what has been missing from the discussion is what drove the Russians to do it, taking such risky steps in the process and exposing themselves to eventual retaliation. It was the Magnitsky Act.

Veselnitskaya had used the retaliatory Kremlin bill as cover, making it appear that the agenda of the meeting was Russian adoption policy. But extensive contact between Russian operatives and members of the Trump team revealed that the Putin regime's priority was sanctions relief. The repeal of the Magnitsky Act would allow Russian kleptocrats to once again use the US to safeguard, invest, and enjoy their stolen wealth.

What the Magnitsky Act did was not only hurt the klepto-crats, but also expose that they were not really patriotic, and that their national pride was a ruse. It speaks volumes that the Kremlin's immediate response was to ban the adoption of Russian children by Americans, essentially retaliating by hurting their own most vulnerable citizens. At the time, Russia had the highest level of orphaned children since World War Two.

The Magnitsky Act is a great model for a piece of legislation that targets regime officials without sanctioning the country or targeting its economy. Russian opposition leader Boris Nemtsov called it 'the most pro-Russian decision taken in the West in many years. It is harmful to Putin's thieves, murderers and scoundrels, and it is beneficial to the country.'[8]

An Integrated Strategy

The success of the Magnitsky Act can guide us towards an integrated strategy for starving and cornering dictatorships that does not misfire and damage their societies in the process. We have led with a long introduction to targeted sanctions, because we believe these will hurt the most—but there's a lot more that can be done. Here's a suggested strategy, in five broad points:

Expanded 'Smart' Sanctions

In 2016, thanks to relentless efforts by Bill Browder and a coalition of organisations, the US Congress enacted the Global Magnitsky Act, which allows sanctioning human rights abusers and corrupt government officials anywhere in the world—not just in Russia. Similar legislation has also been adopted in Canada, the UK, and the Baltic states. This effort should expand, with more countries adopting it, such that smart sanctions come to be enacted across all open societies.

It is not enough to simply pass these acts—it's also important to make them work, impartially. Otherwise, they'll continue to be a political tool applied unequally, suggesting that some human rights abuses deserve punishment, while others can be ignored. The Iranian regime, for example, would be greatly inconvenienced if their key officials and partners-in-corruption were sanctioned by Canada and the UK, where they love to invest and enjoy their wealth. Meanwhile, Human Rights Watch has built a case for sanctioning Saudi Arabia's strongman, Mohammad bin Salman, for his role in Yemen's humanitarian catastrophe, but this has little chance for implementation, since the Saudi regime is seen by many Western countries as a reliable ally, despite its horrific human rights record.[9]

If a dictatorship wants to plunder a country's wealth, it should not be allowed to hoard or spend that wealth in an open, democratic country. This also causes serious damage to the soft power of Western countries, who come to be seen as hypocritical about their values for allowing dictators and human rights abusers to continue to use their economies. The profits brought by these stolen funds only benefit the ultra-rich—meanwhile the cost in terms of the damage caused by these regimes is borne by all. Often, their destruction happens far away in third countries—but it also frequently hits home. A recent example is the 2018 Skripal affair in the UK, where suspected Russian intelligence agents released a highly toxic nerve agent in the city of Salisbury, England, in a failed attempt to assassinate a former Russian double agent for the UK. When allowed space, dictators do not play nice—they only become more empowered and destructive.

More Power to Whistle-Blowers

Projects such as the Panama Papers, the Paradise Papers, the Bahamas Leaks and other attempts to expose financial corruption greatly help the above strategy. Putting information in the public domain allows local journalists and experts around the world to start connecting the dots and following the money trails, exposing more corruption and uncovering more strategies and pathways of kleptocracy. These projects should be given support by democracy-loving people of principle around the world. Even naming-and-shaming alone is sometimes an effective strategy to expose dictators and kleptocrats and force them to change their behaviour.

Universal Jurisdiction

Many serious human rights abusers have been able to get away by hiding behind the cover of state sovereignty. Even the International Criminal Court, established by the UN to prosecute serious war criminals, has its limitations, since its mandate only extends to countries that are party to its founding treaty. In cases where a serious violation takes place outside the mandate of the ICC, the only options are for that country's government to voluntarily accept the court's jurisdiction, or to be forced to via a United Nations Security Council resolution—and we know how that ends. In 2014, for example, Russia and China vetoed a UNSC resolution that would have given ICC prosecutors a mandate to look into war crimes and crimes against humanity committed in Syria.[10]

This is why universal jurisdiction has been proposed as an alternative. According to this doctrine, a victim of serious crime under international law can sue his persecutors anywhere, regardless of where the alleged crime was committed, and regardless of the accused's nationality, his country of residence, or any other relation with the prosecuting entity. Certain crimes are regarded as so grave, and as posing such a serious threat to the entire international community, that states have a right and a duty to prosecute individuals responsible. This includes individuals accused of being implicated in torture, forced disappearances, extrajudicial executions, crimes against humanity, war crimes, and genocide.

Already, Germany and Sweden have taken a leading role in employing universal jurisdiction to prosecute grave violations committed in Syria—both countries have access to a large number of witnesses, thanks to the number of Syrian refugees settled there.[11] Several cases concerning war crimes in Syria have been brought to trial in both countries. In one particular case, an arrest and conviction were made—the perpetrator in question had fled Syria and was in Sweden as a refugee. He had posed in a boastful picture, with his foot on a corpse—and was sentenced to eight months in a Swedish prison. His violation and sentence may seem small in the grand scheme of the Syrian catastrophe, but the case and sentencing present a powerful precedent.

But this is just the start. The judiciary in an open society is marked by independence, ideally sitting above politics and unconcerned by the political mood—and this itself presents an opportunity. It would be good to see universal jurisdiction used further—especially for victims to bring cases against human rights violators who work under governments that are 'friendly' or 'allied' with Western governments. These individuals may never actually be arrested, but a conviction can be what's required for their inclusion on a smart sanctions list, thus making them a subject of targeted sanctions and bans.

Disrupting Propaganda

Dictatorial regimes thrive on propaganda—especially having shut down the space for public debate, dissent, or free speech within their own countries. As we saw with the scandal of Russian interference and fake news during the 2016 US election, these campaigns are often organised from very high up the command chain. While the best way to counter a dictator's propaganda is to provide more avenues for free expression by the people in his own country, it is also important not to allow dictators to use the free speech rights and liberties guaranteed by Western constitutions as a cover for their own propaganda efforts.

This is particularly the case on the global social media platforms that have grown to become a crucial public sphere for millions of people around the world, who lack another avenue of expression. It is ridiculous, for example, that Twitter gives verified accounts to Iranian regime officials, while that same regime denies Twitter access to Iran's own citizens. The same can be said about providing verified Twitter accounts to officials of Gulf states, such as Saudi Arabia, Bahrain, and the UAE, where people are prosecuted, imprisoned, and expelled for expressing their non-violent opinions freely on Twitter. And this doesn't get into other strategies by these regimes, such as the usage of bots, troll factories, and hacking to manipulate global opinion on social media, and to harass activists and researchers. At the very least, their attempts must be exposed—but ideally, they should lose their accounts.

This attitude should also extend to classical media, such as TV, radio, and press publications. A regime that imprisons, tortures, and kills journalists within its own country should not be allowed to run operations in an open society, or to have access to their satellite or cable networks, under the cover of liberal and principled free speech laws. The Iranian regime's Press TV, for example, had its UK licence revoked in 2012 after broadcasting an interview with dissident Maziar Bahari that regulator Ofcom said had been obtained under duress.[12] The Russian regime's Russia Today—which was accused of meddling in the US election—had for years run a subsidiary network in the United States that was only recently asked to register as a 'foreign agent' under anti-propaganda laws. This should extend to other regimes, and not stop short at dictatorships that are seen as friendly allies. If these countries want to use the formidable free speech infrastructures that exist in open societies, they must—at the very least—stop jailing and killing journalists from their own societies.

Consequences for Assisting Human Rights Violators

There's a clear contradiction in the way we treat the supporters of dictators. Supporting a terror group such as ISIS is not allowed in any civilised society, but supporting war criminal regimes that destroyed far more lives is not just allowed—you can get fantastically rich doing it, and face no consequences.

The proposals presented so far will go a long way if implemented, but it's not enough to only target dictators—it's also important to target their support network. This includes other dictators, and, unfortunately, many Western lobbyists, businessmen, and politicians.

Human rights violations do not happen in a vacuum. Smarter sanctions would go beyond targetting individuals who are involved in gross violations—they would also target entities that are deeply implicated in the 'political economy of repression'. This should include providers of both material support and more intangible services, such as public relations and lobbying. The fact that these networks very frequently intersect with other forms of corruption including money laundering and organised crime makes it all the more important.

The same should certainly also extend to weapons contracts and surveillance systems. Countries that supply dictatorships with weapons should automatically be held legally and financially accountable if these dictatorships go on to use them to commit war crimes. Governments of open societies in particular should not have a free hand to provide dictatorships with weapons and security technology and then express regret when they are used for repression. The victims and their families should be able to sue the government that supplied those weapons, regardless of where they are, under the principle of universal jurisdiction.

At this point, such trials are unlikely to have more than PR value—but it is worth remembering that a single breakthrough can go a long way into nudging us towards an institutional shift, whereby enabling gross human rights abuses by dictators is considered to be as criminal as providing material support to terrorism.

Conditional Concessions

There's more that can be done to change the incentive structure governing the behaviour of dictatorial regimes. While kleptocracy is one incentive, dictatorships also care deeply about extending their own rule, eliminating threats to their persons, and tightening their grip on power. If pressured, they will often react by hurting society's most vulnerable. For this reason, it's important when engaging dictators to drive a hard bargain, whereby concessions on key human rights indicators can be won.

Dealing with dictators should be like a hostage negotiation, where calculated concessions are made to the hostage-taker in return for the safety of the hostages. As Oslo Freedom Forum founder Thor Halvorssen says, when dealing with dictators, human rights shouldn't be *on* the table, they should *be* the table.

What would dictators want so badly that they would allow calculated human rights improvements in return? This varies depending upon the current position or predicament of the regime. Where these concessions are sought, they should be carefully selected to make a palpable difference to civil society within the given country. Access to foreign aid, financial loans, foreign direct investment (FDI), key defence or economic treaties, non-aggression agreements, large infrastructure projects, and the lifting of certain sanctions can be used as leverage towards a roadmap that includes freeing political prisoners, reducing pressure on civil society activists, and liberalising free speech laws.

Purists may criticise this as lending a kind of helping hand to dictators; but it's important to remember that any step we take on the road to democracy and human rights is worth it, and makes a difference to people living in these societies. Meanwhile, so-called 'pragmatists' may balk at the idea and question its effectiveness and cost, but it's important to note that this is about the security of the whole world; it's money that you invest today in order not to have to spend more tomorrow on counterterrorism and refugee relief.

Give Them a Golden Parachute

Finally comes the provocative option of giving dictators a chance for a safe exit—for instance, by guaranteeing them a quiet retirement property in exile should they leave. Conditions can be imposed, such as never going into politics again and relinquishing most of their ill-gotten wealth. This is controversial—many would argue that it is a breach of the rule of law and the requirements of transitional justice—but given the amount of damage a threatened dictator can cause, perhaps it should be considered, at least when the dictator hasn't committed certain serious crimes. As we mentioned in Chapter 2, the late Sheikh Zayed of the UAE offered two golden parachutes to Saddam Hussein, which he refused. Another former dictator, Tunisian president Zine El Abidine Ben Ali, accepted a similar offer and retired to Jeddah, Saudi Arabia—arguably, this spared Tunisia a more violent transition to democracy after 2011.

* * *

DEALING WITH DICTATORS

The suggestions we have covered so far form only half of a two-part strategy. It is not enough to pressure dictatorial regimes—it's also important to reach out to their societies.

7

EMPOWERING SOCIETIES

In this chapter, we'll present some ideas about how to empower societies without aiding the dictators who control them. We wish to begin by exploring what gives societies resilience, why civil society activists are important, and how dictators target them and attempt to shut them down. When we talk about the strength and weakness of societies, what exactly do we mean? If we are to accept the premise that dictators are not the true representatives of their societies, then who are the actual representatives?

What Makes a Strong Society?

We're used to reading about the strength of states—this strength is often expressed as economic output, military might, and soft power. What about the strength (or weakness) of societies? A strong society is one that can effectively express its agency and that has the resilience to resist coercion or violence. For a society to be strong, it must have a high degree of cooperation and solidarity between its constituent elements, who should be wise enough to push for their shared interests and their shared values.

The political energy in such a society is expended in pushing 'upwards' together, against systems of oppression and inequality, hence strengthening society even more.

A weak society, on the other hand, lacks the ability to advocate for its own interests or resist bad actors. This is often because it is deeply divided along sectarian, tribal, or racial lines, and hence its energy is dissipated as its constituent elements push 'sideways' against each other. The nature of politics within such a society does not challenge existing power structures—instead, it protects them. The masses do not reach across to one another to oppose institutional injustices, but rather align along ethnic, sectarian, or partisan lines. Meanwhile, the leadership of each sect or tribe is secure and comfortable—it's no wonder that it is to its advantage that this continues.

Narratives of nationalism, sectarianism, and warmongering create more rifts in society and turn elements against each other. (In recent years, this has been facilitated by the rise of social media, especially platforms built on visibility rather than merit, effectively rewarding polarisation and sensationalism.) Weaker societies result in power vacuums that provide opportunities for violent actors to appear, take over, and entrench. It is easier to dominate societies that are kept divided, ignorant, powerless, separated, lacking in any tools of resistance, unable to advocate on their own behalf, and unable to reach out to the world.

In effect, weaker societies are more conducive to the rise of dictatorship. Once dictators are in power, they devote a significant amount of their energy to weakening society further, and keeping it weak. By contrast, strong societies typically have vibrant civil societies, which in turn works to increase the strength and resilience of society as a whole.

In the state versus society dichotomy, dictators want their subjects to believe that civil society doesn't matter, and that the state is in fact the most important agent in society; they'll justify anything in the name of the state, and they'll tell you that they're doing this to defend society. In Egypt, Sisi's supporters have justified massacres, mass imprisonment of political activists, targeting NGOs, and shutting down the space for dissent all in the name of 'survival of the state'. In Syria, Assad's supporters have justified barrel bombs, chemical weapons, and industrial-scale torture dungeons in the name of 'survival of the state'. In their imagination, anything beyond the state is chaos—and they frequently point to terrorist groups as vindication of their view. As we've shown earlier, however, the rise of terror groups is often facilitated by dictators, either by design or through incompetence.

Does this view—that without the strong hand of the state, we get wanton violence—have any merit? To answer this, we should look for what's left behind when the state rolls back—and here, we don't have to imagine.

A scene repeated across the region during the Arab Spring was young people cleaning their own streets, in a gesture that represented their renewed sense of agency and ownership over their cities. This sense of empowerment goes beyond gestures, though—skilled social entrepreneurs can take the helm of change, launching new groups, projects, and initiatives. For the strongest example, and the most painful, we must turn to post-revolution Syria.

What happened when the Assad-led state's control over much of Syria receded in 2011 and 2012, and people were suddenly left to their own devices? Far from a war of all against all, Syrians stepped up and managed their own cities. We saw an explosion of volunteerism and civil initiative—private citizens took up the mantle of running security, operating power plants, cleaning their own cities, and running schools and universities. In key areas, local coordination committees (LCCs) sprouted to organise such activities; in a few areas, local councils were elected, the rebel militants in those areas subjecting themselves to civilian command.

Even as the revolution turned into war, organisations such as the White Helmets sprang up to offer relief, digging people out of rubble after bombings, fixing roads and infrastructure, and providing other services when there was calm. During the darkest days of Aleppo's siege, Syrian activist Marcell Shehwaro ran a network of underground 'bunker schools' in the city. Meanwhile, Raed Fares ran a broad network of workshops, training centres, and a radio station in Kafranbel, northern Syria, even as jihadists closed in. And for years, the citizen journalism group 'Raqqa is Being Slaughtered Silently' operated right under ISIS's noses, at great personal risk and cost.

As the Syrian regime's strategy of turning the revolution into war bore fruit, more and more of these spaces were shut down, and many of these civil society activists became refugees or prisoners, or ended up dead. This was more than just a side effect of the civil war—across the world, dictators are known to target and assault civil society and attempt to debilitate it.

In effect, the sheer ferocity of Assad's assaults following 2011 against Syrian cities that had slipped beyond his control was not meant only to recapture territory, but also to eliminate a powerful counter-narrative: the profoundly threatening fact that vast areas of Syria were able to self-govern outside of his rule. This self-governance would have been impossible without the flowering of civil society in these cities—a civil society that has unfortunately been destroyed.

The most serious challenge to dictators doesn't come from other violent actors—as we've seen, violence helps tyrants to tighten their control further. Often, challenges to dictatorship don't even come from the political opposition. After all, political opposition can be decapitated by targeting or imprisoning its leadership. The opposition can be smeared, co-opted, or exiled, or allowed to take part in a sham political process, in order to give the regime a semblance of legitimacy.

Rather, the most serious challenge to dictators often comes from a strong civil society, including independent activists, journalists, and artists. To maintain control, dictatorships need to keep society stunted, shut down spaces for debate and dissent, impose separation and isolation, spread despair, and ensure that different elements of society live different realities. Civil society activists are often trying to achieve the exact opposite, while gaining trust among the population. It is no wonder, then, that dictators target them.

Independent civil society activists are the best representatives of the creative energy and moral integrity of a society; this is especially the case under dictatorships, where other forms of legitimate representation are missing. No strategy to deal with dictatorship is complete without explicit measures to enable and empower independent civil society.

How Are Societies Empowered?

At the 2014 Oslo Freedom Forum, twenty-one-year-old Yeonmi Park gave a mesmerising speech about how she had fled North Korea. Her escape had been dramatic, but what was even more striking was her description of growing up in the most isolated, insular country in the world, and the moment when her life had changed. It was not a political manifesto or fiery speech that had triggered her awakening, but a romantic movie that we take for granted: *Titanic*. To Yeonmi, the very idea that a man can sacrifice himself for a woman—not for the Party, not for the Great Leader—turned her worldview upside down. She had obtained smuggled DVDs of the film and watched it in secret, hiding under blankets, afraid of being found out.

Dictatorships impose isolation upon their people. It's not always as dramatic as North Korea, but dictatorships always assault civil society, shut down and even criminalise solidarity, and try to keep their people divided and weak. This is why Assad was arresting civil society activists in 2012 even as he released jihadists from jail, and why Sisi's regime has been shutting down public libraries and slapping travel bans on human rights activists. It is also why Saddam banned satellite TV in Iraq, and why Iran's regime bans popular social media platforms today.

One motivation behind such assaults is a fear of losing control over narratives. There's a reason why dictatorships assault bloggers and internet activists—Iyad himself was arrested and then exiled by the Emirati regime for tweets in favour of the Arab Spring and criticising the UAE's support of dictatorship. Others have had far worse fates—the Iranian web developer (and Canadian permanent resident) Saeed Malekpour was sentenced to death in Iran in 2008, on trumped-up charges, in an attempt by the regime to shut down the blogosphere there. His sentence was later commuted to life in prison. In an even more tragic case, Bassel Khartabil, a Syrian internet activist and open source developer, was imprisoned and then executed by Assad's regime in 2015.

Expressions of solidarity have also been criminalised by dictators. The Saudi regime, along with Bahrain and the UAE, criminalised any calls for peace with Qatar during the 2017 Qatar crisis. Dictators need to keep their people distracted through narratives of division and separation, creating more rifts. Cooperative contact between their people and 'others' is considered a threat, or even treason.

And yet, despite all of this separation, or perhaps because of it, people in these societies crave contact with the outside world. We have been to many conferences where normal people from closed societies, whether students, young professionals, activists, or entrepreneurs, come into contact with people from other countries for the first time. The exhilaration and excitement are always memorable, and many are transformed by the experience. A Shia Muslim faith leader with operations in both the UK and

Iraq once told Iyad that there was always a positive result when students who would otherwise study at an Iraqi seminary were given the chance to travel abroad to learn. He laughed as he joked, 'Send them once, and they come back more open-minded. Send them twice, and they come back enlightened. We're afraid to send them again for fear they won't return!'

Cooperative contact does more than just enlighten—it also presents an opportunity to de-otherise, to see 'others' not as adversaries but as friends and colleagues. This is a very powerful measure against extremism, since these experiences can make it very hard for young people to believe that 'everyone in the West hates them', whether told so by their own governments or by terror recruiters. Both dictatorial regimes and terror recruiters frequently call against travelling to the West, calling it corrupt and licentious.

Devising a Strategy

A strategy to empower society has to work on several levels. First, it must foster more contact with diverse people. There can be no solidarity without contact. Second, it must ensure access to information and opportunities. And third, it must increase the visibility of civil society activists. With these in mind, we will share some specific ideas.

Facilitated or Special Travel Visas

The way things are done today, a country that wants to punish a regime denies visas to that regime's citizens. In a glaring contradiction, Trump tweeted his support for Iranians protesting their regime in both 2017 and 2020, even as his 2017 'Muslim ban' continued to deny visas to citizens of Iran.[1] While ordinary citizens of dictatorships are denied travel, holders of diplomatic passports of the same regime can often travel far more freely.

This situation is lopsided—we should be doing the opposite. Talented citizens of countries ruled by dictators should be favoured, rather than hindered, when it comes to travel, immigration, and education opportunities in open societies. Meanwhile, regime officials involved in corruption or human rights abuses, and people with links to them, should be the ones slapped with travel bans. The positive outcomes of this policy, in both the medium and long term, would be well worth it—to start, it would make it clear that our gripe isn't with the people but with their government. The opportunities for cooperative, positive contact, and the potential business brought in by tourists, are additional benefits.

Educational Opportunities

Far from punishing students from countries afflicted with dictatorship by denying them academic opportunities, we should subsidise their education in open societies through providing more scholarships and fellowships. In the Netherlands, the Foundation for Refugee Students (UAF) has since 1948 been providing support for refugee academics; in the UK, the Council for At-Risk Academics (CARA) has since 1933 offered 'a lifeline to academics at risk'. The Open Society Foundations scholarships have also, for years, provided financial support to students from closed societies. These efforts must be expanded and built upon, and they must be made institutional.

Going a step further, we should also look positively at attempts to establish branches of world-class universities in closed societies, as in the case of the Sorbonne University Abu Dhabi and New York University Abu Dhabi. There are many reasons to be critical of these projects, especially how they are used as status symbols by dictators who are actually enemies of free speech and academic freedom. But on balance, the exceptional educational opportunity provided for members of that society is worth swallowing that bitter pill. Of course, this should be conditional upon the university campuses being safe havens for freedom of expression, within reasonable negotiated rules.

As a rule, the question we should ask is: Who's benefitting more, the regime or the society? Or perhaps: We know the regime is deriving a benefit from this, but is the benefit to society worth it?

We'd make the same argument for cultural centres and museums as well, like the Louvre Abu Dhabi and Guggenheim Abu Dhabi. Yes, for the regimes they are status symbols, but for societies, they represent rare assets and opportunities. Again, these agreements should be conditional and negotiated—it makes no sense to have a world-class museum without also guaranteeing free speech within the museum and its related activities. In fact, within closed societies these institutions can be 'free expression safe havens', which the regime is incentivised to tolerate because of their value as status symbols, but which also benefit society and give it breathing space.

Investment Opportunities

We've seen how kleptocracy is the business model of dictatorship, and we've also seen how dictators value access to Western capital, markets, weapons, and security technology. Meanwhile, the economic wellbeing of societies living under dictatorships is often stunted—Middle Eastern countries have some of the world's highest unemployment rates. And while our dictators frequently talk about how they want to improve the economy and create jobs, their record in this regard is dismal, and they seem unwilling to acknowledge—much less tackle—institutional barriers to a free and equitable economy.

A policy of supporting entrepreneurship in closed societies is needed, and it might be something that these dictators are open to, because it helps to boost their economic performance. Venture capital funds and world-class entrepreneurship accelerators can take the lead by opening branches in the MENA or taking part in pilot programmes. Remember, while this is something of a status symbol for these regimes, it also benefits societies greatly and fosters great cooperative contact, especially if it's coupled with a programme of workshops and conferences in which those enrolled can travel and meet like-minded professionals in open societies. These initiatives could also promote cross-regional cooperation—entrepreneurship presents great opportunities to break down barriers and build bridges. Startup accelerators can, for example, facilitate joint workshops between Arabs and Iranians, or between privileged members of society and members of marginalised communities.

A special kind of investment needed would be in cultural products—books, novels, plays, songs, and art—because these things are often stunted and ignored under dictatorships, not least as a result of their assault on free speech and the public sphere. Direct investment in films and books by exiles or refugees is one avenue. But the structural changes in the media and publishing industries present new opportunities—Amazon selling Arabic, Persian, or Kurdish books or Netflix commissioning Arabic or Persian works could be a game changer and can bypass censorship.

Needless to say, the investment opportunities presented should exclude regime officials who are involved in human rights abuses; they should privilege ordinary citizens, especially those from at-risk groups, while under-privileging the already rich and well-connected.

Access to Information

Freedom of speech is democracy's bloodline—that crucial right that, if maintained to any degree, means democracy still has a fighting chance, but if shut down means dictatorship has already arrived. Yet the legal right to free speech is impotent without the tools that allow expression. In the twenty-first century, the single most important medium for both free speech and access to information is the internet. Its importance in societies dominated by dictators has particularly increased with the rise of social media, which provides an alternative public sphere to members of these societies, after the 'real' public sphere—newspapers, magazines, TV, and city squares—has been severely constricted or completely shut down. Social media is where young people in the MENA go to talk, discuss, get informed, and even protest and campaign for their rights. This space is of the utmost importance, and freedom to access it safely must be maintained.

It's no wonder that dictatorships have gone to great lengths to shut down the online public sphere, just like they shut down the original, offline one. The difficulty they encounter, however, is that the online space is far less centralised and not under their direct control. In certain extreme cases, the Middle East's dictators have tried to completely take their country off the internet, as the Mubarak and Gaddafi regimes did during the 2011 revolutions.[2] But these extreme measures are exceptional, and they exact a heavy economic impact—more often, dictators have resorted to censorship, surveillance, propaganda, and going after content creators.

Outright censorship has become much less effective due to the proliferation of technology for circumventing online suppression, and only a few regimes around the world, notably in China, Iran, and North Korea, continue to tightly censor their internet. The preferred strategy for most dictatorships has been to use surveillance technology to identify and target the content creators, meanwhile filling the internet space with their propaganda, employing now-familiar tools such as bots, fake accounts, troll factories, and, when necessary, targeted hacks.

In the particular case of the UAE, the regime has gone to the lengths of spending millions on spyware software, which was used to hack the phone of independent human rights activist Ahmed Mansoor.[3] Mansoor, one of the kindest and most principled voices for human rights in the country, was arrested in March 2017 and sentenced a year later to ten years in prison, under the ridiculous accusation of 'using social media sites to publish false and misleading information that [harms] national unity and social harmony and [damages] the [UAE]'s reputation'.[4]

Needless to say, this assault by dictators on free speech and the public sphere needs to be countered, and people in open societies have a lot of leverage in this area. Even a trickle of information into a closed society can be greatly disruptive; in North Korea, where only the political elite have access to the internet, the Human Rights Foundation (HRF) has pioneered a dramatic project to drop flash drives into the country using balloons flown across the border. The flash drives, donated by volunteers, are loaded with a full offline copy of Korean Wikipedia, e-books, and several subtitled films—like *Titanic*.[5]

Few countries are as isolated as North Korea—and a lot can be done apart from dropping USBs. Large global companies should consider offering subsidised services to users in closed societies, including technology for bypassing government-imposed restrictions. During the 2017 Iran protests, the regime successfully blocked Instagram and Telegram, a messaging app heavily used there for news and communication. Iranian users might have switched to another popular secure messenger, Signal, but couldn't, because the app relies on a crucial Google service that Google had blocked in Iran, due to a particularly strict interpretation of the US sanctions against Iran.[6] Tech companies in open societies should be doing the exact opposite, making it as easy and as safe as possible for users in closed societies to access the internet freely and to defeat government censorship and surveillance.

But importantly, this should be coupled with a strategy that makes it more difficult for dictatorships to use the internet to plan clampdowns on civil society. The sale of surveillance software to dictatorships should be greatly restricted—they often appeal to the 'war on terror' to purchase such software, but then actually use it to target non-violent dissenters and human rights activists. Additionally, as we mentioned previously, social media companies should not be giving dictatorships priority access to their platforms. The 'troll factories' of the Middle East's dictatorships should be exposed and dismantled, and those who assisted, facilitated, or joined these efforts should be named, shamed, and sanctioned.

There is a silver lining, and reason to think that the internet will eventually win. Blockchain-based technologies are bringing a slew of distributed services that are harder to trace and nearly impossible to shut down. A particular attempt that could serve as a model for more innovation is Orchid, an open-source project that effectively allows people in open societies to donate their bandwidth to users living in closed societies.[7] The protocol routes internet traffic randomly through a peer-to-peer network, providing an internet connection free from surveillance and censorship. The creators have claimed that the service would even manage to break through China's formidable firewall.

But we should remember that, while access is very important, there's more that can be done. Free speech restrictions have another insidious effect, which is that they throttle the production of new content in native languages (which is one reason why we're writing this in English). Under the cover of appeals to nationalism, this is often coupled with a war against English, a global language and the language of the internet. The Gaddafi regime in Libya famously banned the teaching of English in schools in the 1980s, and as recently as 2018, the Iranian regime did the same in its primary schools.[8] The effect is that, even when users can access the internet, their options are restricted by the lack of accessible content. To counter this, funding for projects that would translate key online resources such as Wikipedia, Khan Academy, and others into local languages would be hugely beneficial. Free English-language education apps and programmes would also greatly help. We should not allow dictators using the internet to create their own truth unchallenged.

Elevating the Profile of Activists

Some of the most impactful civil society activists in closed societies are completely obscure to a Western audience; working in isolation and obscurity, they are constantly at risk of being targeted by their country's dictators. It is too late to launch solidarity campaigns with these extraordinary individuals after they've been arrested. Efforts should be made to bring them into the global mainstream before that even happens. The more widely known and well-connected they are, the more costly it would be for their regimes to target them. Platforms such as the Oslo Freedom Forum have been doing great work towards this—its events provide an extraordinary opportunity for activists to meet, network, gain media attention, and gain access to policy makers and investors. These efforts deserve to be supported and expanded.

Preparing for the Backlash

In the previous sections, we proposed a dual strategy for holding dictators in check, while also empowering their societies. The hope is that over time, empowering a society and increasing its resilience would allow it to regain its agency and push from within, breaking the cycle of violence, disenfranchisement, and disempowerment.

Once we attempt to change the behaviour of dictators and take steps towards empowering the societies they dominate, the regimes will fight back. It is important to maintain a strategic flexibility, and always to be willing to revise tactics as dictators react. They may, for example, look for other sources of funding or of weapons; or find other tech companies to write their surveillance software. They may try to defeat attempts at encouraging solidarity by issuing travel bans, or by further inflating the divisive narratives of nationalism and sectarianism. They may conduct new forms of disinformation warfare, in order to defeat transparency and communications technology. And they will race to weaponise new technologies, such as blockchain, and subvert them as they did with social media networks. This is why it's important to be adaptable, to have a long-term view, and to use all leverage possible to negotiate a situation where the regimes are incentivised to cooperate and to give their citizens breathing space.

The real hurdle isn't strategy, however—it's political will and mindset. And it's easy to become cynical about this—after all, many Western governments seem to be following the contradictory strategy of supporting human rights defenders while also supporting the regimes that persecute them. In 2014, the Sisi regime imprisoned two Egyptian-American activists, Aya Hijazi and her husband, for the crime of setting up an NGO to help street children—meanwhile, the American government continued to send billions in military aid to the couple's jailers.[9] This situation is unfortunately the rule rather than the exception when it comes to Western-supported MENA dictators.

Disrupting systemic tyranny requires political will, a recognition of how much influence the governments of open societies really have, and a shift in mentality away from the myopic, amoral, and unsustainable mode of thinking that's often falsely presented as 'pragmatic'. It's also important to be principled in this, and to treat all dictatorial regimes as bad for all of humanity. Western governments have so far considered some dictatorships to be trusted allies while treating others as pariahs—this is hypocrisy, and more than being morally repulsive, it also erodes the soft power of these Western democracies. While some dictatorships are definitely more destructive than others, it must be understood that all dictatorships are insidious, and none should be given blank cheques.

The dual strategy outlined in these two chapters won't bear fruit in a few months or a few years, but the hope is that over time and with consistency, civil society leaders will be able to make gains, creating more spaces and increasing social resilience. Success is not guaranteed, but it's worth every effort. What we have proposed has the merit of being non-violent, constructive, and based on impact investments, building bridges, and supporting civil society. Our strategy is human rights-centric, and it does not involve violations of the sovereignty of other countries—although dictators will always, invariably, complain that it does.

And yet the strategy would be incomplete if we didn't plan for another possible outcome: popular revolution. Empowering societies in the face of stubborn dictators can create a situation where dictators are so threatened that they wage war on their own people—or a situation in which the people have simply had enough and break out in protest. Should that happen, there needs to be an explicit strategy of support for the people, and of immediately getting on the right side of history. If a government has helped to empower civil society activists, it should not abandon those activists when their regime assaults them. In these situations, governments of open societies should go 'all in', doing whatever they can to stop the bloodshed.

This discussion is incomplete without talking about the viability of military intervention as a tool in the pro-democracy arsenal. Our analysis so far has made it clear, we hope, that we are generally opposed to foreign intervention, whether through direct military operation or through investing in and legitimising local violent actors. War should generally be avoided, but there are rare instances in which military intervention is necessary. Firstly, there are clear cases where humanitarian intervention is a moral imperative—few would argue, for example, against the military operation that saved Yezidi refugees stranded on Mount Sinjar in northern Iraq, as ISIS fighters closed in on them with genocidal intentions. But even as we acknowledge that these kinds of clear-cut cases are rare, the recent history of conflict in the Middle East makes a strong case that violent actors in the region rarely show restraint. Nothing seems to be off the table—from rape campaigns and enslavement, to industrial-scale torture dungeons, to the usage of chemical weapons on civilian populations. Military intervention in cases where imminent crimes against humanity can be prevented should remain an option, under reasonable parameters.

We understand better than most that the record of military intervention in the region is bleak, and that force should always be a matter of last resort. But there are situations where war criminals cannot be deterred except by force, and a difficult choice must be made. The liberation of Kuwait, for example, is widely seen as having fundamentally been a just cause, despite how it was carried out. NATO's intervention during the Bosnian War also comes to mind as having been necessary in the face of a campaign of genocide. In both cases, military intervention came after diplomatic efforts had failed, ample warnings had been ignored, and multiple international resolutions had been trampled. In both cases, a coalition, not a lone country, took action.

Military operation is like heart surgery—if you need it, it's because you have been going down a bad path for a long time. If you haven't been eating healthily or exercising for years, or even decades, the problem will get severe and urgent enough that it can only be solved with a scalpel. The democratic equivalent of a healthy lifestyle, in this metaphor, would be something like what we described in this chapter—a proactive programme that empowers societies and hinders dictators, increasing social resilience and allowing the population to exercise their agency, ultimately preventing catastrophes.

Another thing that we need to be prepared for is what comes after dictatorship. While increasing social resilience means taking the pathway of gradual but sustained improvement, it is a fact that living under dictatorship exacts a heavy psychological and social toll. Returning to the domestic abuse analogy, imagine an abusive patriarch brutalising his household for decades, until one day they find the courage to gang up on him, restrain him, and force him from the house. Good on them, you may think—but the emotional scars and dysfunctions of decades of abuse don't go away in weeks, months, or even years. Once again, it's important to have a long-term view—ensuring society's resilience can go a long way.

What we presented above are ideas, not plans; they can be critiqued, or expanded upon. But the big picture here is that we need a grand strategy that supports people who live under dictatorship, while limiting the privilege of the dictators themselves and changing the incentive structure around them. While there's a lot that democratic governments can do, the bulk of the work falls upon institutions, companies, NGOs, social entrepreneurs, and activists within both closed and open societies. It is up to those in closed societies to use any space that is made available to them, and it is up to those in open societies to reach out and build tools, programmes, and platforms to help.

The path forward is to reject our dictators but embrace our societies. This, in our view, is what should motivate policy.

What Would It Take?

We laughed out loud while writing these last two chapters, thinking: Are we for real? Advocating for cornering dictatorships at a time when they're most triumphant, and when democracy is in crisis? Advocating for expedited visas for people who live under dictatorship, at the height of the so-called migrant crisis? What world do we live in?

But is all of this simply delusional wishful thinking, or do our proposals make some sense? Some may argue that it's too far out and too expensive—but it's less expensive than a fleet of F-16s, less expensive than aircraft carriers and drone bases, less expensive than two decades of 'war on terror' combined with multiple failed PR campaigns, less expensive than rebuilding countries and providing refugee relief. Most importantly, it's less expensive than the human cost of terrorism and tyranny.

To heal our region would take a far-sighted view that appreciates our world's interconnectedness, and realises that if we allow a wound to fester in one place, it will get infected, and the infection will invariably spread. The greatest crises we face today— economic inequality, terrorism, refugees, climate change, misinformation, and more—are all global in nature, and can't be solved by nation-level thinking. Bringing nation-state solutions to global problems is like bringing a knife to a gunfight.

It would also take a profound understanding of the destructive and insidious effects of dictatorship—how it stunts human potential, crushes native agency, and creates waves of violence and instability. It requires recognition of the fact that 'strongmen' are not true leaders—for true leadership is when you inspire others to follow, not when you coerce and arm-bend them to extract their consent—and that legitimising 'strongmen' in the name of stability only results in more instability, more resentment, and more dictatorship.

It would also take an understanding of the difference between states and societies, and it needs to work towards empowering societies while hindering dictatorships. It would take a recognition that those born in open societies that respect their fundamental human dignity are already privileged, and that they have a moral imperative to help others across the global divide who are struggling to exercise their fundamental rights. Conversely, those of us born in a closed society have a moral imperative to empower ourselves and our communities. But to be privileged and look down on the underprivileged, or to be underprivileged and wallow in victimisation, is immoral.

It would take a profound understanding of the power of solidarity. The dictators have each other's backs and are invested in each other's survival—similarly, civil society activists have to have each other's backs as well. Ultimately, the Middle East crisis factory isn't just a Middle Eastern problem—it's a global problem, with global repercussions. Solidarity should be unconditional, and should not stop at national, ethnic, or religious borders.

It would take realising that democracy isn't a culture or an ideology—ultimately the essence of democracy is a manageable power differential between the ruling elite and the rest of society. A society in which only a narrow elite have all the wealth, education, information, weapons, and international support is a society that's either already deeply dictatorial, or one that's ripe for dictatorship; conversely, a society in which a wide sector has access to economic opportunities, education, information, and international support and solidarity is one that dictatorship will have a hard time subduing. By investing in societies, what we're really doing is closing the power gap between society and the state.

It would take realising that human rights are not about left vs right; they're principles that underlie any political ideology that wants to call itself civilised today. Neither are human rights exclusively 'Western'—if you dig deep into the intellectual and spiritual traditions of any human culture, you find the soul of human rights, a recognition of fundamental human dignity and equality. It's the idea that human beings matter, and that they're endowed with certain basic rights that give them dignity, and that social and political systems should revolve around the recognition and preservation of this dignity.

Above all, it will take courage. Our world today is living through the limbo between the collapse of an old paradigm and the rise of a new one—a period that, in the words of Italian philosopher Antonio Gramsci, is 'a time for monsters'. Now is not the time for unimaginative, managerial thinking that attempts to manage the collapse. It is the time for leaders and testers, for being bold and trying new models and new options, instead of doubling down on what already didn't work.

Ultimately, the real question is, how do you see us, the people of the Middle East? Do you see us as states, or as a bunch of exotic groups of 'others', or instead as fellow human beings? Would you rather respond to hatred and mistrust through more war, more barriers, and more bombs, or through building bridges, expressing solidarity, and embracing our shared humanity?

Should foreign policy focus on the most short-term, unsustainable security goals, or should it reflect a long-term vision? When dealing with dictatorships, should human rights be 'on the table', or should they be the table itself? Must values contradict interests, or should we extend our timeline to the point where our interests match our values without contradiction?

We have aimed to present our analysis of the problem and our advocacy for a solution, which requires a strong resolve and a determination to fight for open society values everywhere. And yet it's easy to become cynical as we read the daily news, seeing the depth of the dysfunction, apathy, lack of leadership, lack of political will, and inability to see beyond the short term. Many seem to have tacitly accepted a slow collapse. It's tempting to be cynical, but it's ultimately a luxury not afforded to those who are directly in the path of this collapse. We can't afford to be cynical. We can't help but advocate—partly out of fear and partly out of hope.

Fear—because we know that things can, and will, get worse. The crisis factory is energised by the global resurgence in illiberal authoritarianism. Dictators are now running around without a leash, causing immense damage and trauma that will take years, if not generations, to recover from. And things are going to get worse; we haven't seen the last or the biggest tragedy. The Middle East is going to be in free fall for a while, and we haven't seen the bottom yet.

Meanwhile, Middle Eastern human rights activists have never felt so abandoned. It seems that every day we get messages from friends who are depressed, looking for an escape, contemplating suicide, or wondering why life is going from bad to worse, when only a few years ago life seemed so hopeful and the future seemed bright.

But we still hope; we still hope that open society values will eventually triumph, and that the pendulum will once again swing back to our side. The other side—the side of the authoritarians—may seem like it's winning, but it's running on lies and fears, and it is ultimately unsustainable.

8

THE NEXT TWENTY YEARS

On 2 October 2018, journalist Jamal Khashoggi stepped into the Saudi consulate in Istanbul to collect papers he needed for his upcoming marriage. His fiancée waited just outside, but Jamal never returned. It was later revealed that he was killed by agents of the Saudi regime inside the consulate. His body was butchered and smuggled to a nearby residence, where it's believed it was burned in a tandoori oven. A source told Iyad that when, hours later, the killers returned to Saudi Arabia on a private jet, they took an ice box with them on board. It may have contained Jamal's head.

Khashoggi was at the time perhaps the most visible Saudi dissident. Having once been a well-respected Saudi journalist and a consultant to the royal family, Khashoggi found himself sidelined after the rise of Mohammad bin Salman and ultimately became convinced he would be arrested. He chose self-exile in 2017, finding a home in Virginia, USA, and a new career at *The Washington Post*.

Jamal's death wasn't the first political assassination by our dictators, nor was it the most brutal. But it marked a turning point in our region's story, as the single most brazen act of political violence against a non-violent journalist by a Western ally in living memory.

After the murder, the usual suspects—particularly the governments of the UAE and Bahrain—lent strong support to Saudi Arabia's crown prince, their propaganda output converging on a unified message. The counter-revolutionary regimes that had intervened to abort democratic transitions in Bahrain, Egypt, Libya, Yemen, and Syria were now closing ranks and signalling that they had each other's backs.

Thanks to President Trump and regional allies, MBS may have escaped accountability, but something fundamentally changed. Among the activists we knew, this change was palpable. Since 2014, our activist community had been beset by divisions over priorities; while some of us concentrated on fighting political tyranny, others thought the focus should be on religious extremism. A few had even believed in MBS's reform narrative. But after the murder, it became impossible to sit on the fence. A new dissident called Iyad to say: 'After Jamal isn't like what's before Jamal. After Jamal, the lines are drawn.'

Perhaps the most notable and lasting change that we experienced was on the international scene. Before Jamal's murder, we had had many extremely frustrating conversations with Western figures about the tyranny of the West's allies—too many wanted to believe that MBS was the 'liberal strongman reformer' that the region needed. The murder changed that instantly and permanently. Overnight, we no longer had to work so hard to make people see these dictators for what they are. The billions spent on the Saudi regime's public image—including MBS's meetings with celebrities in American business, politics, and entertainment—had gone to waste. After the murder, these same figures had to distance themselves from him. MBS learnt the hard way that people do not like it when they are made to look like fools.

THE NEXT TWENTY YEARS

It is a cruel twist of fate that Jamal's murder did more to change attitudes towards the counter-revolutionary axis than its past litany of crimes, including the crushing of the Bahrain uprising, the Egyptian coup, the war in Libya, the war in Yemen, and the arrests of women's rights activists. The truth is that the counter-revolutionary axis had been sick for a while.

In Egypt, the axis's gambit succeeded in reversing the country's 2011 uprising and brought a new dictator—Abdel Fattah al-Sisi—to the region's shrinking family of tyrants. But elsewhere, the counter-revolutionary regional record has been shambolic. In Yemen, a war launched to establish deterrence against Iran-backed militias dragged on, opening the door to more effective Iranian intervention that eventually turned a ragtag tribal secessionist group, the Houthis, into a militia strong enough to challenge Saudi and Emirati advanced Western weaponry. In the process, a humanitarian catastrophe of historic proportions was created.

In nearby Qatar, a blockade and possible attempts at regime change failed miserably, instead leading Qatar to warm relations with Iran and to seek a much closer alliance with Erdoğan, bringing a Turkish base to the Persian Gulf for the first time since the Ottomans left over a century earlier. This is especially significant since Turkey is a contender for leadership of the Islamic world, while Saudi Arabia seems to be retreating from that role.

In Lebanon, attempts to pressure the Saudi-linked prime minister, Saad Hariri, to sideline pro-Iran elements in the government strongly backfired, humiliating and weakening Hariri and strengthening Iran's hand, until the 2019 national uprisings upended internal politics.

In Libya, the axis supported Khalifa Haftar, an authoritarian figure who modelled himself after Egypt's Sisi and consolidated his grip over Libya's east. The country's already-disrupted democratic transition turned into a civil war that soon became a proxy war. Despite support from the axis, as well as from Russia and France, Haftar could not win the war; his frequent failures only opened the door to direct Turkish intervention against him, which would deepen and turn into a rout by mid-2020.

Even the conflict with Iran, whose regime the counter-revolutionary axis had once singled out as especially evil, was mishandled. After the Khashoggi murder, the axis seemed to have out-evilled their Iranian adversaries, and there was a growing sense that they had also failed to stem Iranian influence in the region. After all, the Iranian regime was still entrenched in Syria, Lebanon, and Iraq, was expanding its influence in Yemen, and had achieved a diplomatic breakthrough with Qatar. The confrontation with Iran would be sent back to the US and Israel, with the Americans instating ever-tighter sanctions regimes, and the Israelis carrying out covert operations within Iran.

Perhaps the most damaging thing about this pressure campaign was its effect on the native Iranian protests, which had continued in one form or another since 2017. While many Iranians oppose their regime, many are also patriots and will defend their country if it is targeted. Threats of war aimed at bringing the regime to heel aren't the best way to create a good environment for a democratic transition.

But the most lasting damage that the axis wreaked was arguably in its relationship with the US itself, having invested deeply and recklessly in Trump, perhaps the single most polarising president in America's history. Unlike MENA tyrants, US presidents do not last forever.

Despite these disasters, the axis regimes have been absolutely unable to change course. Dictators do not have the common person's ability to curb themselves or to think about their own future rationally. This is especially the case when they're hysterical and paranoid. Absolute dictatorship is not achieved through institutions—instead, it reflects the personalities, limitations, and irrationalities of a handful of men, surrounded by yes-men who reflect back to them what they want to hear. Faced with setbacks, these tyrants continued to respond from the same playbook—repress, deceive, throw cash at problems, and seek foreign sponsors.

But repression has natural limits—it works, until it doesn't. Under a valid social contract, a large portion of the population might support an autocracy's repressive measures, interpreting them as efforts by the strongman to protect them. But when a regime breaks a social contract and loses legitimacy, repression comes to be seen for what it is—pure thuggery, and an attempt to beat people into submission.

Like fighting bacteria with antibiotics, repression also risks creating resistant strains. Constantly raising the fear barrier can end up creating a resistance movement that is absolutely fearless; constantly pumping out propaganda and disinformation can end up creating a population that is immune to sloganeering and cynical towards propaganda.

Once the social contract is broken, severe repression is more likely to cause further breakage than it is to bring back any sort of sustainable stability. When it comes to struggles for liberty, the illusion of freedom is far more dangerous than coercion. Repression would then create resentment and inspire resistance, rather than convincing a population to accept their lot.

We can't place ourselves in the heads of our adversaries, so we don't know how they really feel about their strategic position in early 2021. But we would not be surprised if they actually believe they are winning. After all, when you're in free fall, it sometimes feels like you're flying. The dictators are in an existential battle, and you can't afford to lose an existential battle. They have a limited handbook of responses and seem unable to step outside it. They've already burned too many bridges to have a way back. Their persistence isn't a sign of conviction, but of strategic rigor mortis; they continue to double down because there is no plan B.

But if we were in their shoes, we wouldn't be able to help but feel a sense of foreboding that a once-familiar world was coming to an end.

A World Is Ending

There's another reason why the dictators repeatedly reach for the same handbook—it's because for the longest time, it has worked. Now, in the post-2011 MENA, and especially the post-2018 MENA, there's a sense that what has worked forever has stopped working—that a world is not just changing, but ending.

Much of our book has been about legitimacy, but while legitimacy is the crux of the story, it's not the only factor at play. There are other global trends interacting with it in important ways, changing the world in which this battle for legitimacy is being fought. We have explored many of these trends in previous chapters, including changes in demographics, education, communications, and connectivity. But there is another important one to note.

The world is moving beyond fossil fuels; while they were once overwhelmingly valuable, with climate change has come a period of transition away from them. Oil's peacetime prices are years past their peak in 2008. At the same time, the world's superpower, the United States, became a net exporter of oil for the first time in November 2019.[1] This is a crucial development given that the US has for decades enabled the worst excesses of oil-rich MENA dictatorships in order to protect its own energy security.

Shifts in the geopolitics of energy are also situated within larger global trends. While Western nations continue to be prosperous and powerful, the world is becoming far less Western-dominated than it has been for centuries, with other countries catching up. Moreover, new social media platforms have brought many native voices such as ours into the global conversation about the region— a development that did not exist two or three decades ago.

The global levelling has not only happened between world regions, but within them as well. Members of previously marginalised communities are managing to reach positions of power, prestige, and prominence globally. The previously silenced are finding a voice and are using their platforms to draw attention to the injustices and inequalities that their communities have for generations been subjected to, without being able to tell their story. All of this has meant that today's young people are increasingly progressive in their outlook, upending the twentieth-century political and ideological status quo and pushing for more equality and inclusion.

In the US, the country's demographics are marching inexorably towards a point in time when whites will no longer be a majority—according to Census data, this could be as soon as 2045.[2] The intense polarisation in US politics cannot be separated from this demographic anxiety; this is a country where historically, power has been tied to race. At the same time, decades of foreign wars have produced a knee-jerk revulsion among many Americans towards entanglements abroad.

For a long time, a number of petty dictatorships in our region have been able to act with impunity because they felt they had the unconditional support of the world's only superpower. They never felt a need to establish legitimacy by consent of their people. After the 2011 upheavals, they believed they could act like superpowers themselves and rearrange a region of half a billion people to ensure democracy never comes. Now, the foundations of this unconditional support are being pulled from underneath them. And on their own, they have little real leverage, and a limited toolkit of responses.

For Israel, too, an old world is coming to an end. Gone are the days in which it could present itself as a lonely liberal state encircled by regressive enemies; Israel has become a hegemon among its neighbours, and regionally most of its major existential threats have been eliminated. Once hailed as 'the only democracy in the Middle East', it is now surrounded by native uprisings calling for democracy across the region. The majority of these pro-democracy protesters do not look upon it kindly and consider it to be a force of oppression. At the same time, young American Jews, like many other members of their generation, are increasingly progressive in their values, bringing many of them to sharply criticise Israel for its now-permanent occupation and subjugation of the Palestinians.

Starting in August 2020, in the dying months of the Trump presidency, a series of normalisation agreements were signed between Israel and key Arab dictatorships. First was the United Arab Emirates, whose de facto leader, Mohammad bin Zayed, is a central figure behind the counter-revolutionary axis. Second came Bahrain, in a gesture that could not have happened without buy-in from Saudi Arabia. Meanwhile, Saudi Arabia is strongly expected to follow suit, with multiple public gestures and year-long leaks about secret contact and collaboration.

For Israel, these agreements mark a diplomatic and strategic breakthrough, but for the Arab dictators, the stakes are much higher. The new coalition is explicit in its aggressive posture towards the Iranian regime and, less directly, the Turkish regime. Iran and Turkey have a combined population of over 160 million; in comparison, the UAE has just over 1 million citizens, and Bahrain just over 600,000. While the UAE faces few internal threats, its dependence upon migrants makes it extremely susceptible to foreign threats. Migrants make up 90 per cent of its population, and any war would result in a migrant exodus from which its economy could not recover.

Meanwhile, the Bahraini regime sits atop simmering tensions, having survived an uprising in 2011, as a country with a long history of native uprisings. In Saudi Arabia, on the other hand, normalisation of relations with Israel would mean ceding its position—and soft power—as a leader of the Sunni world; it would also lead to further splits in a royal family that is already fractured thanks to MBS's power consolidation moves since 2015. But MBS seems to have calculated that he needs foreign sponsors, now that America's support is no longer reliable.

In pursuing foreign backing, the regimes continue to play regional politics as though they are big powers, despite their fragility, small size, and precarious strategic situation. Rather than seeking to cool down regional tensions, they opted to raise the stakes. Faced with a changing world and a deepening crisis of legitimacy, they chose to diverge even further from popular will; the results of the 2019–2020 Arab Opinion Index showed that only 6 per cent of Arab publics would support diplomatic recognition of Israel by their country.[3]

Forgotten among all of this was the plight of the Palestinians, whose post-1993 leadership put all its eggs in the basket of 'land for peace': an end to Arab states' rejection of relations with Israel in return for its withdrawal from occupied territories. The normalisation agreements mark the end of this paradigm—in place since 1967—and with it the end of Palestinian aspirations to statehood. A few Israelis, too, sense the danger; the end of the Palestinian state spells the end of liberal Zionism, which could lead to the end of Israeli democracy. The agreements present to the world an illusory peace, which in reality is based upon little more than cynicism, opportunism, fundamentalism, and tyranny.

The Great Collapse

The MENA is home to over 500 million people—that's more than the population of the European Union, and far more than the population of the United States. The majority of regimes in this vast region are not sustainable. A day of reckoning for each is coming, sooner or later; today's 'unsustainable' is tomorrow's crisis. For decades, most of the MENA was hostage to a regional order that met every crisis by doubling down. But while the Western analyst looking at the MENA in the early 2020s would be excused if they saw nothing but devastation and despair, we do not pin any hope on this order.

We started this book's narrative by speaking about how the MENA's post-colonial order stumbled from one broken promise and legitimacy crisis to another until it ran out of lies. In this broader context of a failed regional order, the Arab Spring wasn't an event that happened in 2011, but a thirty-year intergenerational transition that happens to have begun in 2011. A new generation has arrived, and what the generations before them considered good enough is no longer good enough. This transition will not be linear. Some actors that appear to be the winners now may not even exist by the time this is over.

This recalls Gramsci's words from nearly a century ago: 'The old world is dying, and the new world struggles to be born: now is the time of monsters.' We have had our own share of monsters, and monsters do not die quietly.

Side by side with the rise of this new generation is a slow-motion collapse of the region's order. A decade after 2011, not a single regime in the region is sustainable, many having passed up several chances for serious reform to dig a deeper hole, thinking that if they simply eliminate all options other than themselves, they win by default. Unfortunately for all of us, all that does is eat away at the region's foundation, bringing us closer to collapse.

We'll be honest—we're ambivalent about this collapse. Imagine that you and your family are locked for years in a prison building, enduring occasional torture and with no hope for escape. Then, the prison itself starts to fall in, the earth moving from underneath it. Imagine how you'd feel—part afraid that the collapse will kill you and your loved ones; part hopeful about a chance for freedom. This is how we feel about the collapse of the MENA's regional order, a collapse that has already started and is past the point of no return. This order destroyed many lives when it was standing, and as it falls apart it's destroying more lives.

There was no hope that the order would resolve its legitimacy crises and deliver to us what we want—a life of dignity. There is no hope now that the order can be reformed. There's no hope that the collapse can be stopped. We gave up all hope in that order long ago. We have to place our hope beyond that order. It's collapsing anyway—let it come crashing down so we can have a shot at a life of liberty.

What will the next twenty years look like? We think it will look like more of the same. Across the region, we see an ecosystem of crises: political stagnation, authoritarian consolidation, native uprisings; civil wars, proxy wars, terror waves; failed revolutions, successful revolutions; interrupted transitions, successful transitions. There are refugee waves, but there is also smarter organising. There's massive trauma, but also human resilience. This is itself situated within a wider global collapse of twentieth-century politics, international norms, old economic models, and the so-called 'liberal world order'.

We submit to you that this is exactly what a regional, intergenerational democratic transition looks like.

We remind you of what Europe's own intergenerational transition to democracy looked like—it took thirty-one years, involved two World Wars, and resulted in 100 million deaths and the largest genocide in recorded history. Even after that, Europe's democratisation was incomplete and had to wait until the fall of the Berlin Wall and its aftermath.

History in the twenty-first century seems to march much faster than it did in the nineteenth and twentieth centuries, and we hope that our region is spared the worst human tragedies of this transition. This is a geopolitical event of enormous importance, when a region's half a billion people gain their political agency for the first time. It will not be easy, or fast, or pretty—but never bet against history.

Despite the death and collapse around us, we live in a world in which much that is new is being born. There is great pain, but there is also great reason for hope. And hope often springs from despair.

A New Hope

It was from the depths of darkness that the spring returned eight years after Mohamed Bouazizi set himself on fire, blossoming in a second wave in late 2018. Over the next year, there were uprisings in Sudan, Algeria, Iraq, Lebanon, and Iran, as well as significant protest movements in Egypt and Jordan. The MENA's *ancien régime* had spent the years since 2011 repressing their citizens, chasing dissidents, inciting civil strife, and pouring gasoline on the region's wars—they had done nothing to address the underlying reasons that led people to revolt.

The showdown was different. The regimes of the counter-revolutionary axis were more alert and more aggressive than they had been in 2011. They had thought that they could create a region in which uprising was impossible, in which people were 'taught a lesson' and would always be scared stiff of the misery visited on those who revolt. 'Do you want your country to become like Syria or Libya?' they asked. But the people's answer was loud and clear—they organised smarter, and their narrative was firm and mature: Syria and Libya were broken not by their people but by their dictators, who had chosen to destroy their countries rather than cede power. And the response to forces who are itching to shed blood is to maintain a heroic level of non-violent discipline.

When the uprisings came back, they came back with a vengeance. Limited protests had started in Iran, where native resistance had simmered since 2009, with an escalation in 2017, its pace reducing but continuing into 2018. In March 2018, a protest movement started in Gaza, which had been under a stifling Israeli blockade since 2007. In June 2018, a brief but sharp protest movement took hold in Jordan, leading the government to resign. In December 2018, mass protests broke out in Sudan. In February 2019, major demonstrations spread across Algeria. In September 2019, limited but notable protests returned to Egypt. In October 2019, protests erupted in Iraq, and two weeks later in Lebanon. By November, nationwide protests were taking place in Iran.

Each of these uprisings reflected local grievances and demands, but there were important commonalities that cannot be ignored. Economic difficulty, corruption, autocracy, and lack of accountability topped the list of grievances in most of these movements; non-violence was the main strategy of the protesters in all of them. And the leading demand by the mostly young protesters was to have a life of dignity—to feel like they mattered and that they had a future to look forward to, rather than a picture of endless stagnation and crushing compromise.

Near the Gaza border fence, mass demonstrations demanded the right of return for Palestinian refugees (a majority of Gaza's inhabitants are refugees from elsewhere in historical Palestine). Crucially, the protest organisers adopted non-violent strategies and narratives, despite attempts by both Hamas and the Israeli authorities to hijack the narrative.

In Sudan, protests quickly evolved into a revolution that overwhelmed the government's ability to repress it. The country had been ruled since 1989 by Omar al-Bashir, an Islamist dictator; his thirty years in power saw violence, corruption, repression, economic stagnation, worsening public services, and systemic human rights abuses. The uprising was disciplined and strategic, led by a coalition that included Sudanese political parties, resistance committees, and perhaps most importantly an umbrella group of trade unions called the Sudanese Professionals Association. In April 2019, Omar al-Bashir was deposed in a coup. The protesters were savvy, and unlike their Egyptian comrades in 2011 did not shout, 'The people have removed the regime'; instead, they chanted, 'The revolution has only begun.' Sudan entered a transitional period, which has involved both ongoing political violence and negotiations, and in which regional forces, notably the UAE and Saudi Arabia, continue to attempt to intervene.

In Algeria, protests started days after Abdelaziz Bouteflika, the country's president since 1999, announced that he would be running for another term. Bouteflika had led the country since the end of its decade-long civil war, and his twenty years in power had seen corruption, unemployment, a shrinking political and public space, and increased army influence in the economy. Algeria's 2019 protests were large and persistent, and successfully prevented another presidential run by Bouteflika. Even after that accomplishment, protesters continued to press for full democracy and a complete end to military control of the country's economy and government. The uprising was remarkable in its non-violence—not surprising, given the country's recent history of violent civil war.

Egypt's September 2019 anti-corruption protests were relatively sparse, but notable. The post-2013 regime had raised the barrier of fear, repression, and disinformation to a level it thought was unscalable, but corruption revelations by a whistleblower led to street protests. Eight years after the toppling of Mubarak, and six years after Sisi's coup, the familiar chant of 'The people want the fall of the regime' was back on Egypt's streets—albeit briefly; the government managed to regain control of the streets within a few weeks and arrested over 4,000 people, including several notable lawyers, journalists, academics, and activists.

Uprisings in Iraq and Lebanon started in October 2019—while Egypt's protests were still ongoing—and would prove far larger and more persistent. In Iraq a failed state, captured by sectarian parties and further damaged by militias, had led to rampant corruption, unemployment, and poor public services. Young protesters—many born after the American invasion—took to the streets demanding an end to the post-2003 political system that they had lived under all their lives. A surge of native Iraqi nationalism saw the youth repudiate sectarian divides and rally behind their shared Iraqi identity—rejecting foreign influences from both the US and Iran. The response from the government—and especially from militias backed by the Iranian regime—was a massacre. By January 2020, over 700 protesters had been killed, with over 27,000 wounded.

In Lebanon, protests started over the introduction of new taxes but quickly escalated into a national uprising. Lebanon had seen a destructive sectarian civil war that ended only in 1989 with the establishment of a 'sectarianised democracy' in which political power was shared among the country's eighteen recognised confessional groups. Now, protesters rallied behind their Lebanese identity, calling for an end to the sectarian-based political system that had brought rampant corruption, economic stagnation and inequality, unemployment, foreign intervention, and a breakdown in basic services. In a particularly rousing moment, hundreds of mothers from across confessional groups rallied against violence, marching and chanting: 'My child must not die for anyone.' The Lebanese civil war had lasted fifteen years and left over 100,000 dead and over a million displaced.

Meanwhile, Iran's November 2019 uprising was the country's most serious escalation of civil resistance in years, coming as the Iranian regime and its militias were already nervous, given the protests in Iraq and Lebanon—two countries where their entrenched proxies have enjoyed decades of impunity. In a familiar pattern, protests started over economic conditions but quickly escalated into calls for the end of the regime, of Iran's isolation, and of its expensive foreign adventures in the region. The protesters used a combination of tactics, including peaceful sit-ins and demonstrations, as well as arson attacks on government facilities. The regime responded with extreme violence, with up to 1,500 killed and over 7,000 arrested.

When Covid-19 spread across the region in early 2020, many of these movements were still ongoing, with continuing campaigns in Sudan, Algeria, Lebanon, Iraq, and Iran. The pandemic hit pause on most of these protests, thanks to a combination of lockdown rules and the onset of further economic hardship. It is too soon to know where the second wave of uprisings will land, especially given the extremely complex political landscape in most of these countries, and the rising regional tensions.

But already, this revolutionary wave has had a much better success rate than the first. The 2011 wave saw protest movements in twenty countries; ultimately, four regimes fell and one was so severely damaged that it lost regional relevance. By contrast, during the 2018–2019 wave, protests in six countries saw two regimes fall with two others still caught in existential crises. Sudan and Algeria are moving towards democratic transition, however imperfect. The worst-case scenario of a civil war was successfully averted, partly because of the prior lessons the protesters had learnt from, as well as their strict adherence to non-violence.

It's important to note that while the Algerian, Sudanese, Iraqi, and Lebanese uprisings of 2019 were fully native and independent, they would have been so much more unlikely had the 2011 uprisings not succeeded in rearranging the region's geopolitical realities. For example, we would not have been celebrating successful democratic transitions in Tunisia, Algeria, and Sudan if a triumphant Gaddafi and Mubarak were still in power, ready to help their buddies.

The impact can be enormous. Before these uprisings, about 1 in 35 citizens of the Arabic-speaking MENA lived in a free democracy. If the Algerian and Sudanese democratic transitions are successful, that figure will go up to 1 in 8. Whoever wants to discount successive future waves—with smarter tactics and better success ratios—will do so at their own peril.

The Decades Ahead

Many years ago, a much younger Iyad was talking to a much younger Ahmed. In discussing the future of our MENA region, Iyad used an analogy from Isaac Asimov's *Foundation*. In the classic science fiction series, a scientist predicts that the Galactic Empire is collapsing, something that will result in a 30,000-year period of savagery. But, if the right measures are taken, that dark age will only last for 1,000 years.

The MENA's regional order is collapsing. It will be catastrophic. We can't prevent that collapse, and nor is preventing it our task. Our task is to build what comes next. And, in doing so, to reduce the period of savagery in between.

This is both a strategic and a moral imperative. What does justice look like when you're surrounded by catastrophe? Will you have the luxury to sit and mourn? Not really—you have to pick yourself and your comrades up, and start building. This is also what we expect of our allies: not to legitimise the collapsing order or normalise the collapse itself, but to work with us to ameliorate its worst effects and accelerate the rise of a better MENA—one without tyrants, terrorists, or foreign intervention.

We don't want to minimise the depth and scale of the trauma that's being created across our region. We understand that healing will be difficult—you can't brutalise a society for two or three generations without that society becoming dysfunctional. Countries ruled by some of the most corrupt and vicious dictators on the planet cannot be expected to function well the day after they've gone. Healing will take time, and much effort.

As we look into our future, we acknowledge that our adversaries have a few things going for them, despite the many trends eating at the foundations of their power. The counter-revolutionary axis has large cash reserves, an economy that offers short-term opportunities, a preferential relationship with the West, and most importantly a world order that still privileges dictators, regardless of their human rights violations. But among the best things they have is something for which we are responsible—we, the opposition, have not yet organised effectively enough, and have not come up with formidable enough alternatives that can reclaim legitimacy for our people.

Despite all the dictators' posturing, we continue to top their list of threats. This is still a battle for legitimacy fought through narratives. The suffocation of free speech, destruction of public spheres, and severe repression of activists is the tyrants' attempt to win this battle by ensuring we don't even show up. They have used their highly advanced hacking technology not against their regional adversaries, but to hack journalists, dissidents, and human rights activists.

These are the imperatives for our work as we navigate the next twenty years—to build power for our societies and with them, to help our people write the story of their past and their future, and to facilitate healing in a region ridden with trauma. As our dictators look for foreign sponsors, we must remember that the fate of the MENA will be decided by its people, not by the benevolence of any US president or foreign power. It is our responsibility to centre our own people, because if we don't, nobody will.

As we reach the last few pages of this book, we want to send a message to the reader. People tend to adjust to the horizons of political possibility. When a dictator's grip seems to be strong and his rule sustainable, even those who are repulsed by his crimes will temper their expectations. We're here to tell you that the region's dictatorships are in trouble, and they will not be around forever. We are also here to remind you that we too are human beings, and we deserve to live in freedom and dignity, to choose our own rulers, and to speak our minds freely. Lastly, we want to impart that we come from an ancient region with a long memory—we do not forget those who stood with us, and we do not forget those who stood with our persecutors.

A Bold New Region

The ideas behind the MENA's decade of uprisings were both powerful and simple: If you want to govern me, it has to be by my consent, not by your guns. Those who govern should be accountable to those they govern. People shouldn't suffer for things they did not choose. Power should always serve justice, not the reverse. Everybody deserves to live in dignity, and nobody can live in dignity if they do not have their freedom. We deserve better. A series of defeats and a turbulent century tried repeatedly to sell us defeat and to convince us that we do not deserve any better. But if there's one idea that keeps coming back, screaming, it's that we deserve better.

These ideas, of course, are not unique to the MENA; they represent all of us and our joint struggle. Across the world, there is an ever-strengthening fight for equality, justice, and progressive ideals; this struggle is not between cultures, but within them. It is a struggle between those of us everywhere who want to coexist, and those everywhere who want to fear, hate, and repress. A new, wonderful world is being born—we are the future. Despite the catastrophic scenes and the crisis factory, we are the future. Global authoritarianism is rising, but we hope that our efforts in this struggle will mean that this is not their new renaissance, but their last stand.

In this book, we mostly referred to the Arabic-speaking regions of the MENA, but we want to stress that we reject twentieth-century Arab Nationalism and conceive of our region as so much more. Our region of concern is the entire MENA region, which defies all conventional classifications—geographic, ethnic, or religious. While it is a cradle of world civilisations and faiths, its modern history is traumatic, as it became a crisis factory and a playground for tyrants, terrorists, and foreign powers. These bad actors have dominated narratives about the region— the tyrants want to boost hyper-nationalism, and divide the already divided; the terrorists want to paint the entire region black; meanwhile foreign powers berate our 'regressive culture' even as they arm and cover up for our tyrants.

It is no wonder that many within our region have fallen into cynicism and despair. So many have given up on broadening their circle of concern beyond the borders imposed by the modern nation-state. Yet, we dare to speak of the region as a whole, rather than individual states, separated and in conflict. To us, this is a region of over half a billion, made up of multiple peoples who each have their own identity, but are united by an intersection of history, faith, culture, and political experiences and ambitions. The MENA is Arab and Persian and Turkish and Kurdish and Amazigh and more; it's Sunni and Shia and Christian and Jewish and more.

So long as we support each other's subjugation, we'll all live under one boot or another. So long as we refuse to embrace each other, we'll keep living in fear and isolation, and we'll keep looking for 'protectors' who will rob us blind while inflicting trauma on everybody and murdering our future. We're not safe until we're all safe, and we're not free until we're all free.

* * *

Somewhere in our collective consciousness is this tendency to expect 'real truths' to be bitter and painful—even unpleasant.

Similarly, we have a tendency to expect that if something is cosy, soothing, and makes us feel warm inside, it must be a comfortable illusion.

Here are some truths. Love is all that matters, and it's what makes everything worth it. Not many people appreciate just how difficult it is, after paying a heavy personal price, to insist on being fuelled by love and not revenge. To be pulled to the future by a beautiful vision, rather than pushed forth by your pain and your demons. Either our activism is fuelled by love, or we won't get very far or achieve very much as activists. Our job isn't only to battle dictators and make them nervous. It is also to be a wellspring of support, solidarity, and love for every human being who dreams of freedom. We will never give up on our region, and we will never give in to our dictators.

Hope, we must stress, is far more profound than optimism. Hope doesn't depend on things working out. Hope is the sense that some things are truly worth our life's work, regardless of the outcome. And, in that sense, we're brimming with hope.

NOTES

FOREWORD

1. Ronald Reagan, *An American Life*, New York: Simon and Schuster, 1990.
2. https://obamawhitehouse.archives.gov/the-press-office/remarks-president-cairo-university-6–04–09.
3. http://time.com/4180526/what-obama-gets-wrong-about-conflict-in-the-middle-east.
4. http://www.pewglobal.org/2017/06/26/tarnished-american-brand.

INTRODUCTION: AN UNLEARNING

1. MBZ also demonstrates that you can be both a Muslim and an Islamophobe. Islamophobia is a fear of Muslims—and those whose day job is subjugation of Muslim masses and denying them political agency are doing so out of a fear of Muslims.
2. https://www.nytimes.com/2018/07/27/sunday-review/obama-egypt-coup-trump.html.
3. https://arabist.net/blog/2017/11/13/the-arab-world-is-not-ready-for-complacency.

1. BROKEN PROMISES

1. The exact number depends on which measure is used—Freedom House's rankings are available here: https://freedomhouse.org/report-types/freedom-world.
2. https://muse.jhu.edu/article/174006/summary.

211

3. The other state often described as a democracy in the Middle East is permanently occupying another people. We do not think military occupation is very democratic.

4. Raja Club Athletic chant: https://www.youtube.com/watch?v=LY9R KaW4iqE. Translation by Iyad El-Baghdadi.

5. We are aware that any attempt to tell the story of political legitimacy across such a wide region in a single chapter will involve some simplifications and omissions; we nonetheless hope that the resulting insights are worth these sacrifices.

6. Composed by Tunisian poet Beshir Laribi. Translation by Iyad El-Baghdadi.

7. The exact figure is disputed, with estimates ranging from 300,000 to 1.5 million.

8. https://www.ias.edu/ideas/beginnings-authoritarian-culture-arab-world.

9. In future decades, other movements sought less radical means for integration; the Gulf Cooperation Council was formed in 1981, and the Arab Maghreb Union in 1989.

10. Ahmed Fouad Negm, لا صوت يعلو فوق صوت المعركة ('No Voice Is Above the Sound of the Battlefield'). Translation by Iyad El-Baghdadi.

11. Available in Arabic: http://archive.aawsat.com/leader.asp?section=3& issueno=10002&article=358711,

12. https://uil.unesco.org/case-study/effective-practices-database-litbase-0/ literacy-training-and-employment-women-algeria.

13. https://www.jstor.org/stable/1187367?seq=1.

14. A composite measure of health, education, and income, which is designed to measure average achievement in basic dimensions of human development.

15. http://www.arab-hdr.org/data/indicators/2012–54.aspx.

16. https://data.worldbank.org/indicator/SE.ADT.LITR.ZS.

17. Samuel Huntington, *Political Order in Changing Societies*, New Haven: Yale University Press, 1968.

18. Osama Bin Laden, 7 October 2001. Translation by Ahmed Gatnash.

19. Osama Bin Laden, 7 October 2001. Translation by Ahmed Gatnash.

2. THE VICIOUS TRIANGLE

1. https://www.france24.com/en/20090901-maliki-blames-syria-attacks-assad-denies-claim-.
2. Hassan Hassan and Michael Weiss, *ISIS: Inside the Army of Terror*, New York: Phaidon Press, 2015.
3. https://www.thedailybeast.com/assad-henchman-heres-how-we-built-isis.
4. https://deeply.thenewhumanitarian.org/syria/articles/2014/12/11/understanding-the-drivers-of-radicalization-in-syria.
5. https://www.telegraph.co.uk/news/2016/04/25/isils-deal-with-bashar-al-assad-and-the-40m-a-month-oil-profits.
6. https://www.middleeasteye.net/news/assad-government-has-infiltrated-islamic-state-says-syria-diplomat.
7. John Kirby, Spokesperson, Daily Press Briefing, US Department of State, 7 October 2015: https://publications.atlanticcouncil.org/distract-deceive-destroy/assets/download/ddd-report.pdf.
8. Mohamed Soltan, interview with Ahmed Gatnash, 13 February 2018.
9. https://timep.org/wp-content/uploads/2018/07/TIMEP-ESW-5yrReport-7.27.18.pdf.
10. https://www.bbc.co.uk/news/world-middle-east-33955894.
11. https://www.middleeasteye.net/news/end-lockdown-egypts-north-sinai-brings-limited-relief-residents.
12. https://www.brookings.edu/blog/markaz/2015/08/07/sisis-regime-is-a-gift-to-the-islamic-state.
13. Mohamed Soltan, interview with Ahmed Gatnash, 13 February 2018.
14. https://www.hrw.org/news/2017/09/06/egypt-torture-epidemic-may-be-crime-against-humanity; https://egyptindependent.com/nineteen-new-prisons-built-egypt-2011-rights-group.
15. https://www.buzzfeednews.com/article/borzoudaragahi/unfairly-accused-of-being-an-isis-member.
16. https://www.aljazeera.net/encyclopedia/events/2011/5/6/%D8%B1%D8%B3%D8%A7%D9%84%D8%A9-%D8%A7%D8%B9%D8%AA%D8%B0%D8%A7%D8%B1-%D8%B5%D8%AF%D8%A7%D9%85-%D8%AD%D8%B3%D9%8A%D9%86-%D9%84%D9%84%D9%83%D9%88%D9%8A%D8%AA.

17. https://www.thetimes.co.uk/article/the-secret-downing-street-memo-xh9h29xhqzr.

18. Barack Obama, *The Audacity of Hope: Thoughts on Reclaiming the American Dream*, New York: Crown Publishers, 2006.

19. Najib al-Nuaimi, *I Knew Saddam Hussein*, Al Jazeera English (31 July 2007).

20. https://theintercept.com/2015/03/02/brief-history-netanyahu-crying-wolf-iranian-nuclear-bomb.

21. https://www.vox.com/2015/2/26/8114221/netanyahu-iraq-2002.

22. https://www.independent.co.uk/news/world/middle-east/israel-stepped-back-brink-war-iran-2010-8282741.html.

23. https://www.huffpost.com/entry/obama-and-irans-rouhani-m_b_3478925.

24. https://www.washingtonpost.com/lifestyle/style/obama-official-says-he-pushed-a-narrative-to-media-to-sell-the-iran-nuclear-deal/2016/05/06/5b90d984–13a1–11e6–8967–7ac733c56f12_story.html.

25. Maryam Nayeb Yazdi, interview with Ahmed Gatnash, 16 January 2018.

26. Roya Boroumand, interview with Ahmed Gatnash, 2 February 2018.

27. James McCormick, *The Domestic Sources of American Foreign Policy: Insights and Evidence*, Lanham, MD: Rowman & Littlefield Publishers, Inc., 2018.

28. https://www.theguardian.com/world/2018/feb/18/netanyahu-israel-ready-act-against-dangerous-iran-munich-speech.

29. https://www.vox.com/2016/3/1/11127424/trump-authoritarianism#fear.

30. https://georgewbush-whitehouse.archives.gov/news/releases/2003/09/20030909.html.

31. https://www.aljazeera.com/news/2003/10/22/iraqi-resistance-looks-set-to-intensify.

32. https://edition.cnn.com/2003/US/04/11/sprj.irq.pentagon.

33. https://www.independent.co.uk/news/world/middle-east/paul-bremer-iraq-ten-years-we-made-major-strategic-mistakes-i-still-think-iraqis-are-far-better-8539767.html.

34. https://edition.cnn.com/2005/WORLD/meast/01/30/iraq.audit.

35. https://www.theguardian.com/world/2007/jul/13/usa.iraq.

36. https://www.theguardian.com/world/2010/oct/22/iraq-war-logs-military-leaks.

37. https://www.nytimes.com/2003/02/15/world/threats-and-responses-bin-laden-s-message-to-muslims-in-iraq-fight-the-crusaders.html.

38. http://content.time.com/time/specials/packages/article/0,28804,1967340_1967342_1967422,00.html.

39. https://www.independent.co.uk/news/media/al-qaida-turns-jihad-into-war-by-media-321848.html.

40. https://middle-east-online.com/en/time-finally-ran-out-%E2%80%98atiyah%E2%80%99.

41. https://www.aljazeera.com/news/2009/12/12/us-iraq-jail-an-al-qaeda-school.

42. https://www.theguardian.com/world/2014/dec/11/-sp-isis-the-inside-story.

43. Ibid.

44. https://nypost.com/2015/05/30/how-the-us-created-the-camp-where-isis-was-born.

45. Jean-Pierre Filiu, *Gaza: A History*, London: C. Hurst & Co., 2014, p. 206.

46. https://www.lrb.co.uk/the-paper/v28/n06/john-mearsheimer/the-israel-lobby.

47. Avi Shlaim, *The Iron Wall: Israel and the Arab World*, London: Penguin, 2014.

48. https://www.nytimes.com/1995/11/12/world/zeal-of-rabin-s-assassin-linked-to-rabbis-of-the-religious-right.html.

49. https://www.theguardian.com/world/2020/oct/31/assassination-yitzhak-rabin-never-knew-his-people-shot-him-in-back.

50. https://www.timesofisrael.com/netanyahu-bats-away-claims-he-incited-to-rabins-murder.

51. Lisa Goldman, interview with Ahmed Gatnash, 17 February 2018.

52. https://www.nytimes.com/2001/11/17/world/senators-urge-bush-not-to-hamper-israel.html; https://www.congress.gov/congressional-record/2002/5/2/house-section/article/h2078–2?s=1&r=28.

53. https://www.al-monitor.com/pulse/originals/2012/al-monitor/israeli-security-fence-architect.html.

54. https://www.idf.il/en/articles/palestinian-terror/setting-the-facts-straight-on-the-security-fence.

55. https://edition.cnn.com/2004/WORLD/meast/07/09/israel.barrier/index.html.

56. https://oldwebsite.palestine-studies.org/resources/special-focus/palestinian-prisoners.

57. https://www.972mag.com/ziad-abu-ein-wanted-2015-to-be-the-year-of-non-violent-struggle.

58. https://www.vice.com/en/article/8gexmg/issa-amro-hebron-court-case-israel-nonviolent.

59. Chris Hedges and Laila Al-Arian, *Collateral Damage: America's War against Iraqi Civilians*, New York: Nation Books, 2008.

60. https://www.theguardian.com/news/2016/aug/09/life-and-death-in-palestine.

61. James Fallon, *The Psychopath Inside: A Neuroscientist's Personal Journey Into the Dark Side of the Brain*, New York: Current, 2013.

3. BREAKAGE

1. Barry Mirkin, 'Population Levels, Trends and Policies in the Arab Region: Challenges and Opportunities', United Nations Development Programme, Regional Bureau for Arab States, Arab Human Development Report Research Paper Series, 2010.

4. RISE OF THE AXIS

1. https://eng-archive.aawsat.com/theaawsat/interviews/a-talk-with-peninsula-shield-force-commander-mutlaq-bin-salem-al-azima.

2. https://www.washingtonpost.com/news/monkey-cage/wp/2017/07/03/how-egypts-generals-used-street-protests-to-stage-a-coup.

3. https://foreignpolicy.com/2014/11/06/why-i-still-believe-in-the-arab-spring.

4. https://www.middleeasteye.net/news/fin-coo-coo-uae-envoy-mocks-saudi-leadership-leaked-email.

5. https://www.nytimes.com/2017/11/20/world/middleeast/saudi-arabia-corruption.html; https://www.nytimes.com/2017/11/23/opinion/saudi-prince-mbs-arab-spring.html.

6. https://www.newyorker.com/magazine/2018/04/09/a-saudi-princes-quest-to-remake-the-middle-east.

7. https://www.france24.com/en/20171030-qatar-emir-accuses-blockade-countries-wanting-regime-change.

8. https://www.theguardian.com/media/2017/jul/01/demand-al-jazeera-closure-shows-how-much-enemies-fear-it.

9. https://www.hrw.org/news/2017/09/15/saudi-arabia-prominent-clerics-arrested; https://www.hrw.org/news/2018/05/18/saudi-arabia-womens-rights-advocates-arrested.

10. https://www.theguardian.com/technology/2020/jan/21/amazon-boss-jeff-bezoss-phone-hacked-by-saudi-crown-prince.

11. https://twitter.com/_2us/status/153094746586365952.

12. https://www.aljazeera.com/news/2017/8/20/saudi-twitter-users-urged-to-expose-qatar-sympathisers.

13. https://www.hrw.org/news/2017/09/15/saudi-arabia-prominent-clerics-arrested.

14. https://www.businessinsider.com/saudi-arabia-crown-prince-mohammed-bin-salman-us-trip-meetings-2018–3.

15. https://www.hrw.org/news/2018/11/20/saudi-arabia-detained-women-reported-tortured.

16. https://www.cbsnews.com/news/saudia-arabia-expels-canadas-ambassador-recalls-own-row-over-womens-rights-activists-arrests.

17. https://twitter.com/iyad_elbaghdadi/status/1026784740278456321.

18. https://www.nytimes.com/2011/03/15/world/middleeast/15bahrain.html; https:/www.nytimes.com/2019/04/09/us/politics/trump-abdel-fattah-el-sisi.html; https:/www.nytimes.com/2019/04/26/world/africa/sudan-revolution-protest-saudi-arabia-gulf.html; https:/www.nytimes.com/interactive/2018/10/26/world/middleeast/saudi-arabia-war-yemen.html.

5. THE VITALS

1. https://www.imf.org/-/media/Files/Conferences/2018/morocco-conference/PDFs/jobs.ashx.

2. https://www.ilo.org/global/about-the-ilo/multimedia/maps-and-charts/WCMS_212431/lang—en/index.htm.

3. https://www.economist.com/briefing/2016/08/06/look-forward-in-anger?fsrc=permar%7Cimage3.

4. https://www.imf.org/-/media/Files/Conferences/2018/morocco-conference/PDFs/jobs.ashx.

5. https://en.wikipedia.org/wiki/List_of_Arab_League_countries_by_GDP_(PPP), accessed 21 December 2020. Data from https://www.imf.org/en/Publications/SPROLLs/world-economic-outlook-databases.

6. https://oec.world/en/profile/country/sau; https://oec.world/en/profile/country/dza; https://oec.world/en/profile/country/egy.

7. https://data.worldbank.org/indicator/SL.AGR.EMPL.ZS?end=2020&locations=ZQ&start=2010.

8. https://www.dohainstitute.org/en/Lists/ACRPS-PDFDocument Library/Arab-Opinion-Index-2019–2020-Inbreef-English-Version.pdf.

9. http://arabcenterdc.org/policy_analyses/the-arms-trade-in-the-mena-region-drivers-and-dangers.

10. http://statisticstimes.com/ranking/democracy-index.php.

11. http://rsf.org/en/ranking.

12. Arab Human Development Report 2016, http://hdr.undp.org/sites/default/files/reports/2699/ahdr2016en.pdf, p. 176.

13. https://www.dohainstitute.org/en/Lists/ACRPS-PDFDocument Library/Arab-Opinion-Index-2019-2020-Inbreef-English-Version.pdf, p. 17; https://www.globsec.org/wp-content/uploads/2020/06/Voices-of-Central-and-Eastern-Europe-read-version.pdf, p. 13.

14. https://www.dohainstitute.org/en/Lists/ACRPS-PDFDocument Library/Arab-Opinion-Index-2019–2020-Inbreef-English-Version.pdf, p. 23.

15. Frantz Fanon, *The Wretched of the Earth*, Harmondsworth: Penguin, 1967 [1961].

16. Barry Mirkin, 'Population Levels, Trends and Policies in the Arab Region: Challenges and Opportunities', United Nations Development Programme, Regional Bureau for Arab States, Arab Human Development Report Research Paper Series, 2010, p. 13; https://data.worldbank.org/indicator/SP.DYN.TFRT.IN?locations=ZQ.

17. https://www.middleeastmonitor.com/20190417-report-finds-quiet-revolution-in-middle-east-birth-rates.

18. https://www.unicef.org/mena/reports/profile-child-marriage; https://databank.worldbank.org/reports.aspx?source=283&series=SP.DYN.SMAM.FE.
19. https://ourworldindata.org/literacy.
20. http://ftp.iza.org/dp11385.pdf.
21. https://ourworldindata.org/grapher/correlation-between-education-and-democracy.
22. https://www.internetworldstats.com/stats5.htm.
23. https://www.popcouncil.org/uploads/pdfs/2010PGY_SYPEFinalReport.pdf, p. 139–40.

6. DEALING WITH DICTATORS

1. http://fortune.com/2017/07/29/vladimir-putin-russia-jeff-bezos-bill-gates-worlds-richest-man.
2. https://www.foxbusiness.com/money/jeff-bezos-mbs-net-worth-crown-prince.
3. http://www.businessinsider.com/qaddafi-200-billion-richest-2011-10.
4. https://www.theguardian.com/world/2011/feb/04/hosni-mubarak-family-fortune.
5. http://www.middleeasteye.net/news/ali-abdullah-saleh-yemens-64-bn-man-749430825.
6. https://www.thedailybeast.com/from-chubby-basketball-fan-to-fratricidal-maniac-how-swiss-boarding-school-shaped-kim-jong-un.
7. https://www.washingtonpost.com/politics/trump-dictated-sons-misleading-statement-on-meeting-with-russian-lawyer/2017/07/31/04c94f96-73ae-11e7-8f39-eeb7d3a2d304_story.html.
8. http://www.worldaffairsjournal.org/blog/vladimir-kara-murza/russian-lawyer%E2%80%99s-%E2%80%98trump-mission-was-dump-magnitsky-act.
9. https://www.hrw.org/news/2017/12/19/its-time-un-sanction-saudi-arabias-crown-prince.
10. https://news.un.org/en/story/2014/05/468962-russia-china-block-security-council-referral-syria-international-criminal-court.
11. https://www.hrw.org/report/2017/10/04/these-are-crimes-we-are-fleeing/justice-syria-swedish-and-german-courts.

12. https://www.bbc.co.uk/news/entertainment-arts-16652356.

7. EMPOWERING SOCIETIES

1. https://uk.reuters.com/article/uk-iran-rallies-usa/trump-republican-allies-endorse-iranian-protesters-idUKKBN1EP0JI; https://www.politico.com/news/2020/01/11/trump-iran-protesters-tweets-097554.
2. https://www.nytimes.com/2011/01/29/technology/internet/29cutoff.html; https://uk.reuters.com/article/us-libya-protests/libya-cuts-off-internet-service-network-monitor-idUSTRE71G0A620110219.
3. https://www.nytimes.com/2019/03/21/us/politics/government-hackers-nso-darkmatter.html.
4. https://www.amnesty.org.uk/free-activist-detained-blogging-uae.
5. https://flashdrivesforfreedom.org.
6. https://www.theverge.com/2018/1/2/16841292/iran-telegram-block-encryption-protest-google-signal.
7. https://www.orchid.com.
8. https://www.bbc.co.uk/news/world-africa-23524134; https://www.theguardian.com/world/2018/jan/07/iran-bans-teaching-english-primary-schools-official-says.
9. https://www.reuters.com/article/us-egypt-usa-aid/u-s-military-aid-for-egypt-seen-continuing-despite-rights-concerns-idUSKCN0T22E520151113.

8. THE NEXT TWENTY YEARS

1. https://www.forbes.com/sites/arielcohen/2019/11/26/making-history-us-exports-more-petroleum-than-it-imports-in-september-and-october/?sh=7f34ccee5f3b.
2. https://www.brookings.edu/blog/the-avenue/2018/03/14/the-us-will-become-minority-white-in-2045-census-projects.
3. https://www.dohainstitute.org/en/Lists/ACRPS-PDFDocument Library/Arab-Opinion-Index-2019–2020-Inbreef-English-Version.pdf, pp. 55–6.

ACKNOWLEDGEMENTS

Far more people's efforts went into making this happen than I could possibly do justice to, and I hope those not mentioned here will graciously forgive me when I realise my oversights.

Firstly, thanks to Usman Asif, whose hospitality enabled work on this book to restart after a long hiatus, and to Nasser Weddady, whose encyclopaedic knowledge and guidance were available to us at every turn.

Thanks to Thor, Alex, and the Oslo Freedom Forum team, for making it more possible for human rights activists to understand each other's struggles and transcend regional boundaries, and to Jamila Raqib and Maryam Nayeb Yazdi, for helping me to know what that actually means beyond warm fuzzy feelings.

My thanks to Maryam, Mohamed Soltan, Roya Boroumand, and Lisa Goldman, whose insightful interviews on the events they experienced informed our telling of the story of the region.

I'm grateful to my friends and loved ones for keeping me sane during this process, and especially to my father and grandfather, for vividly recounting the slow pain of two generations of broken promises in our region—you've seen it all before, but I hope our generation lives up to your expectations.

And my everlasting gratitude to every person who struggles to make the world a fairer place—those efforts inspire me every day.

Ahmed Gatnash

ACKNOWLEDGEMENTS

Ahmed's list is better than mine, and I'd like to offer my thanks to everyone he has acknowledged above.

Writing this book has been quite a journey; it started when Giuseppe and Antonia Laterza gave a refugee a book contract, all the way back in 2016, and when Toby Mundy became my agent shortly afterwards. Thank you for believing in me.

My sincere thanks to my friends Zaynab, Belabbes, Nasser, Jamila, Maryam, Thor, and Åsne, who had a great impact on my thinking about my struggle and the world. When we agreed or when we disagreed, you helped me to think more clearly and inspired me to become a better person.

I'm grateful for my wonderful community on Twitter, who never failed to stimulate my thinking, push back on my ideas, and keep me honest. And for every activist whose passion and ideas pushed us to hone our own.

I'm grateful to my very Palestinian parents, who raised me with a strong sense of identity and dignity. And for my loved ones who went through this journey with me: Laila, Ammara, Ziad, and Ismael.

And last but not least, my immense gratitude to Farhaana Arefin, the world's best editor. Thank you for your passion, your patience, and your perseverance. We couldn't have done this without you.

Iyad El-Baghdadi

INDEX

223

INDEX

INDEX

terrorism in, 47, 56–63
trade union movement, 102
Twitter in, 125
United Arab Republic (1958–71), 29
English language, 140, 179
Enlightenment (c. 1637–1800), 23
Erdoğan, Recep Tayyip, 6, 191
Estonia, 156, 157
ethnic cleansing, 10
European Union, 140

Facebook, 100, 105
Fahd, King of Saudi Arabia, 38
Fallujah, Iraq, 81
Fanon, Frantz, 142
Fares, Raed, 170
Fighting Terrorism (Netanyahu), 72
financial crisis (2008), 100, 102
FLN (Front de libération nationale), 27
football, 61
foreign aid, 16, 64, 163
foreign intervention, xiii–xiv, xvi, xvii, 12, 17, 46, 64–99
    cutting and leaving, 7–9
    democracy, spreading of, 77
    dicatorships and, 64–78
    legitimisation of tyranny, 12, 14, 16, 17, 40, 64–77, 131, 150
    terrorism and, 78–99
forever wars, 98
Foundation (Asimov), 205

Foundation for Refugee Students, 174
Fourteen Points (2018), xv
France, 8, 11, 23, 26, 27, 107, 141, 192
free movement, 10–11, 27
Free Russia Foundation, 153
free speech, 17, 34, 140, 160–62, 176–80
    in Egypt, 58–9, 60
    in Saudi Arabia, 124–6, 128–30
    in Syria, 50
    in UAE, 118
Free Syrian Army (FSA), 48, 51, 54
Freedom and Justice Party, 4–5, 56
French Revolution (1789–99), 107, 141
Friedman, Thomas, 122
Friends of Syria, 55

Gaddafi, Muammar, 29, 33, 41–2, 99, 111, 152, 177, 204
Gates, William 'Bill', 127, 152
Gatnash, Ahmed, ix, xv, 150, 205
Gaza, 89, 90, 93, 109, 201
genocide, 160, 183, 199
Germany, 160
Ghazzawi, Razan, 49
Ghoneim, Wael, 100
Ghouta chemical attack (2013), 52, 112
Global Islamic Resistance Call, The (al-Suri), 84

228

INDEX

INDEX

INDEX

INDEX

INDEX

INDEX

INDEX

INDEX

INDEX

INDEX